THE WORLD'S **60** BEST

BURGERS

PERIOD.

THE WORLD'S 60 BEST

BURGERS

PERIOD.

ABOUT THIS BOOK

The 60 burgers in this book are, *in our opinion*, the 60 best burgers in the world. Our team of chefs, writers and gourmets explored everything the culinary world has to offer to create this collection of the world's 60 best burgers.

We based our recipes on the following criteria:

QUALITY OF INGREDIENTS
ORIGINALITY
TASTE
APPEARANCE
SIMPLICITY

Are these our personal favorite burgers? Of course! But rest assured, our team of passionate, dedicated gourmets put time and loving care into formulating and testing each recipe in order to provide you with the 60 best burgers ever. In fact, our chef brought each freshly made burger straight from the kitchen into the studio— no colorants, no sprays, no special effects added—and after each photo shoot, our creative team happily devoured the very burgers you see in these photos.

We hope you'll enjoy discovering these recipes and using this book as much as we enjoyed making it.

TABLE OF CONTENTS

CREDITS 002

ABOUT THIS BOOK 009

INTRO 017

FLAVOR & COST LEGEND 018

A SHORT HISTORY OF THE BURGER 021

MUST-HAVE TOOLS 023

TIPS & TRICKS 025

HOW-TO GUIDE 027

GLOSSARY 029

THE CHEF'S SECRET 031

THE CLASSIC WITH FRIED SHALLOTS 032

LAMB & ROASTED RED PEPPER BURGER 034

BURGER WITH JACK SAUCE 036

PULLED PORK BURGER 038

LAMB, PANCETTA & ROASTED GARLIC 040

PORK BURGERS WITH GREEN APPLE SLAW 044

THE BARBARIAN 046

DELUXE B.L.T. 048

THE CHIP SHOP BURGER 050

THE BACON SURPRISE 052

PROSCIUTTO TILAPIA BUNDLES 056

AL PASTOR BURGER 058

CRISPY CHICKEN CRUNCHBURGER 060

CAJUN SHRIMP BURGER 062

TOTAL TOFU 064

THE JAMAICAN 068

VEGGIE PORTOBELLO BURGER 070

GARLIC BUTTER EXPLOSION 072

THE BREAKFAST BURGER 074

THE COFFEE COWBOY 076

THE AUSTRALIAN 080

VEGGIE BLACK BEAN BURGER 082

THE SLOPPY JOE 084

CHICKEN SOUVLAKI BURGER 086

WELSH RAREBIT BURGER 088

MINI CRAB CAKE BURGER 092

PORK, ZUCCHINI & JALAPEÑO 094

THE OKTOBERFEST 096

MERMAID CROQUETTE 098

PORK & SHRIMP WITH PINEAPPLE SALSA 100

CHICKEN PARMESAN BURGER 104

SALMON CILANTRO BURGER 106

DUCK, HAZELNUT & MANGO 108

THE FOUR CHEESE BURGER 110

LAMB, BACON & BLUE CHEESE SAUCE 112

THE ROSSINI BURGER 116

LAMB PITA BABA 118

MINI BLUEBERRY COCKTAIL BURGER 120

PORK SCHNITZEL BURGER 122

GREEN & BLUE BURGER 124

THE PORTUGUESE 128

CHICKEN CURRY BURGER 130

BRAISED BEEF & RED WINE 132

THE VIETNAMESE 134

VADA PAV BURGER 136

VOLCANO BURGER 140

MINI TURKEY BURGER WITH GUACAMOLE 142

DUCK & FOIE GRAS BURGER 144

TURKEY & SWEET POTATO 146

BURGER WITH CREAMY ARTICHOKE SPREAD 148

RINGSIDE BURGER WITH PORT SAUCE 152

THE MEXICAN 154

RACLETTE BURGER 156

THE ITALIAN 158

FALAFEL BURGER 160

THE STEAMROLLER 164

MUSHROOM BARBECUE BURGER 166

2 IN 1 BURGER 168

THE MOROCCAN 170

THE EMPIRE BURGER 172

INGREDIENTS INDEX 176

SAUCES, SPREADS, GARNISHES & SIDES 180

CONVERSION CHART 187

INTRO

Every one of the 60 best recipes in this book features a flavor and cost legend (see pages 018 and 019) to guide your taste buds as well as your wallet in choosing the perfect dish. You will also find a glossary of culinary terms (page 029), handy cooking tips and tricks (page 025), and a list of must-have kitchen tools (page 023) that will help you create the world's BEST recipes. Finally, use the easy-to-follow Table of Contents (pages 010 and 011) and Ingredients Index (pages 176 to 181) to find everything you're looking for.

Impress guests with your food knowledge from our informative "Did you know?" sidebars, and take your meals to the next level thanks to our tasty tips and serving suggestions!

Bon appétit!

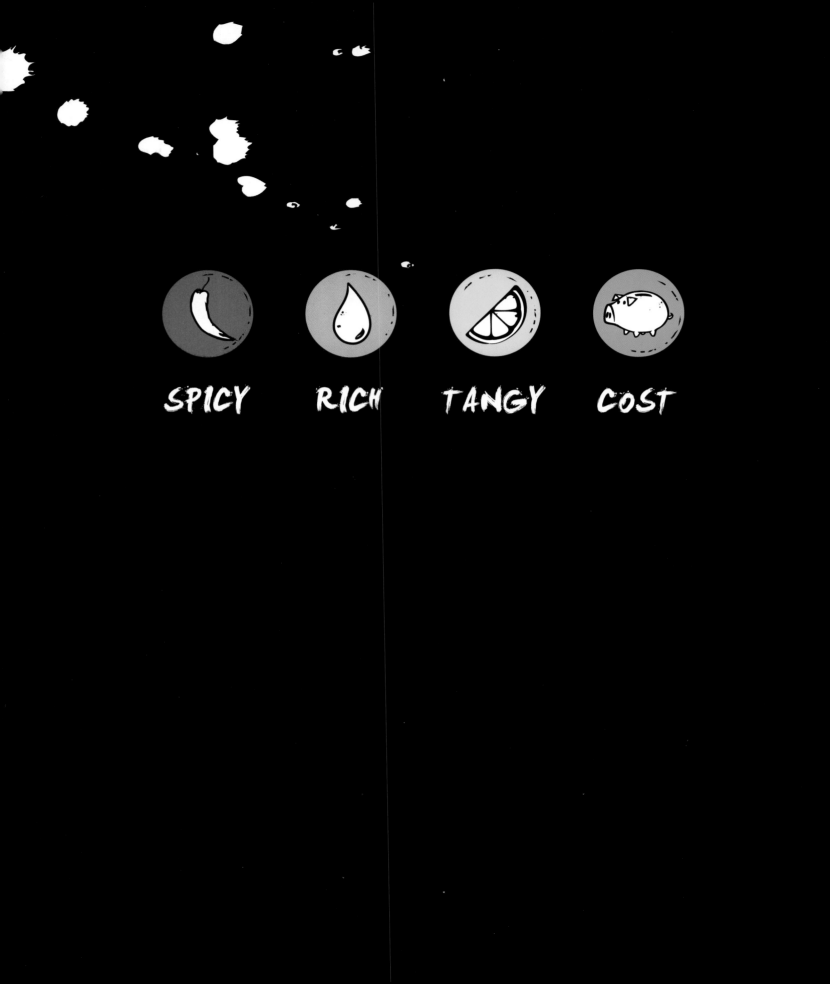

LEGEND

HOT • PEPPERY • ZESTY

LOW   MEDIUM   HIGH

CREAMY • BUTTERY • LUSCIOUS

LOW   MEDIUM   HIGH

ACIDIC • LEMONY • VINEGARY

LOW   MEDIUM   HIGH

COST OF INGREDIENTS

LOW   MEDIUM   HIGH

A SHORT HISTORY OF THE BURGER

The hamburger first appeared on American menus in the early 19th century. These days, a hamburger is generally defined as a hot sandwich consisting of a ground meat patty placed inside a sliced roll.

But the true history of the hamburger goes all the way back to the 12th century, when the Mongols were waging their campaign to conquer the world. These fierce horsemen had little opportunity to stop and cook food, so they placed ground meat under their saddles when riding into battle. After the Mongols invaded Moscow, their unique method of preparing meat was quickly adopted and adapted and became the dish we know as steak tartare (Tartars being the name the Russians gave to the Mongols).

Eventually, the dish made its way from Hamburg, Germany to the United States, and *Hamburg steak*, or *hamburger*, became a standard meal among immigrants and the lower classes. Interestingly, the German term *hamburger* is no longer used in Germany; the patty is called *frikadelle* or *bulette*, words borrowed from the Italian and French. Jewish immigrants in New York continued to prepare meat in this style, and its popularity quickly spread across the continent. By the middle of the 20th century, the hamburger had become an iconic symbol of American cuisine.

Nowadays, a burger is so much more than a plain beef patty between two slices of bread. It can be made with beef, pork, fish, chicken, tofu, veggies, or legumes and topped with every kind of cheese, sauce and condiment imaginable. So fire up the barbecue, pick up your tongs and get flipping!

MUST-HAVE TOOLS

WHAT YOU NEED TO MAKE THE WORLD'S BEST BURGERS

1. A **whisk** for making mayonnaise

2. A **mandoline** for perfectly julienned vegetables

3. A **barbecue** or **grill pan** with a ridged surface for grilling burgers and toasting buns

4. A **hand blender** for making pesto or easy mixing

5. A **chef's knife** for chopping, cubing, dicing and mincing

6. A **large frying pan** for cooking

7. A **large spatula** for flipping burgers

8. A **small pot** for making sauces and chutneys

9. A quality **pair of stainless steel tongs** for cooking burgers like a true grill master

10. A **pastry** or **basting brush** for brushing oil onto patties and buns

11. A **zester** or small grater for zesting citrus fruits

TIPS & TRICKS

FOR CREATING THE WORLD'S BEST BURGERS

1. The key to making the best burgers is using only the best ingredients.

2. The best burgers are homemade. Restaurant burgers are often made in a hurry and don't get the love and careful preparation they should.

3. The ideal burger size is 3/4 lb.

4. Making your own burgers isn't just about creating new flavor combinations; it's also about experimenting with colors, aromas and textures.

5. As the saying goes, to each his (or her) own. Everyone has a different opinion about what makes a tasty burger!

6. Attention carnivores: veggie burgers are burgers too!

7. Put those utensils away—the best way to eat a burger is with your hands.

8. If you believe that burgers can't be a part of a healthy diet, think again. Just serve your favorite salad made with fresh vegetables on the side.

9. Eating burgers is supposed to be messy! Make sure to keep a stack of napkins handy for you and your guests.

10. Take inspiration from your favorite recipes to make YOUR very best burger.

HOW-TO GUIDE

COOKING YOUR BURGERS TO PERFECTION

How do you know how long you should cook your beef burgers? It depends on where and how you purchased your beef. Beef that has been ground in-store or at a processing plant must always be cooked well done to ensure that all bacteria are killed to prevent food poisoning. If you prefer your burgers cooked to medium or medium-rare, prepare your ground beef at home with either a knife or grinder, or have it ground by your butcher. Make sure the meat is fresh and cook it immediately after grinding.

Chicken, turkey, pork, and sausages must always be fully cooked through.

Here are four easy ways to cook the world's best burgers:

1. **ON THE BARBECUE**
   Cook patties on the lower grill over high heat. The burgers' internal temperature must reach 160°F (70°C). Finish cooking on the upper grill if burgers start to burn.

2. **IN A FRYING PAN OR A GRILL PAN WITH A RIDGED SURFACE**
   Sear patties over high heat and finish cooking in a 400°F (200°C) oven.

3. **IN A NON-STICK FRYING PAN**
   Les burgers plus fragiles comme les burgers de poisson ou de légumineuses ont avantage à être cuits dans une poêle antiadhésive.

4. **BY FRYING IN OIL**
   To prevent delicate burgers like fish or bean burgers from falling apart during cooking and flipping, use a non-stick frying pan.

REMEMBER :

- Don't press down on your burgers during cooking—they will lose their natural juices and end up dry.

- To check if your burgers are fully cooked, use the poke test: medium-rare is yielding, medium is semi-firm, and well done is firm.

- Cooking time will vary according to the cooking temperature and the thickness of your burgers.

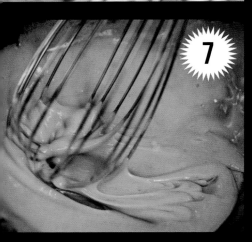

GLOSSARY

1. SEASON

To improve the flavor of a dish by adding salt and pepper to taste.

2. BLANCH

To cook vegetables briefly in boiling salted water.

3. BRUNOISE

A basic knife cut in which food is cut into very small cubes, about 1/8 inch.

4. DICE

A basic knife cut in which food is cut into cubes.

5. DEGLAZE

To remove and dissolve caramelized bits of food at the bottom of a pan in order to make a jus or a sauce.

6. THINLY SLICE

To cut into thin, equal slices.

7. EMULSION

A mixture of two or more liquids or substances that normally can't be combined. An emulsifier such as egg yolk or mustard is often added to prevent separation.

8. CHOP

To cut into small pieces with a sharp instrument (knife or food processor).

9. REDUCE

To thicken a liquid by evaporation over heat.

10. JULIENNE

A basic knife cut in which food is cut into long thin strips. A mandoline is often used for this cut.

11. SEAR

To cook in fat (butter or oil) at a high temperature to obtain a golden or brown crust.

12. ZEST

To remove the zest (outer skin) of citrus fruits with a zester, grater, or peeling knife.

THE CHEF'S SECRET

Every seasoned chef will attest that the real secret to creating a successful dish is to *taste! taste! taste!* Taste before and after seasoning, add some heat or a squeeze of lemon juice if you think your dish needs a little kick, or go ahead and double the herbs or even the cheese! The most important thing is to follow your instincts and your senses. Listen for that telltale sizzle, inhale the tantalizing aromas, and CONSTANTLY taste your food so you can get to know your dish in all its stages.

There you have it—the simple secret to creating delicious, original dishes.

THE CLASSIC WITH FRIED SHALLOTS

SERVES 4

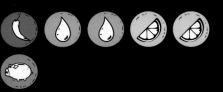

FOR CLASSIC BEEF BURGERS

1 lb ground beef
1 egg
2 tbsp bread crumbs
2 tbsp steak spice
2 tbsp ketchup
2 tbsp shallots or chives, finely chopped
Freshly ground pepper

FOR MAYONNAISE

1 egg yolk
1 tbsp Dijon mustard
Juice of 1/2 lemon
3/4 cup (180 ml) vegetable oil
Salt and freshly ground pepper

FOR FRIED SHALLOTS

4 shallots, thinly sliced
Canola oil for frying

TOPPINGS

4 slices cheddar cheese
4 slices bacon
4 slices tomato
8 slices pickle
Choice of condiments

4 burger buns

PREPARATION

Combine burger ingredients. Form 4 patties and refrigerate.

For mayonnaise : In a bowl, whisk together the egg yolk, mustard, and lemon juice for 2 minutes. Add oil in a steady stream, whisking constantly until it turns into mayonnaise. Season with salt and pepper.

For fried shallots : In a large heavy-bottomed pot, heat 1 1/2 inches vegetable oil and fry shallots in small batches until golden brown. Remove from oil with a slotted spoon and transfer to a paper towel to drain.

Cook bacon. Cook patties for 5 to 6 minutes on each side. Top with cheddar cheese slices and allow cheese to melt.

Toast buns. Spread mayonnaise on bun bottoms and top with patties, bacon, condiments, and fried shallots.

2

LAMB & ROASTED RED PEPPER BURGER

SERVES 4

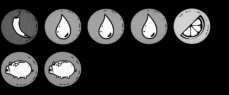

 **DID YOU KNOW?**

Piri-piri sauce is a spicy and fragrant Portuguese chili sauce that is commonly used as a marinade for the famously fiery *rango grelhado com piri-piri*, or grilled chicken with piri-piri sauce.

FOR LAMB BURGERS

1 lb ground lamb
2 tbsp chives, chopped
2 tbsp bread crumbs
2 tbsp steak spice
1 egg

TOPPINGS

2 red peppers
1 tbsp olive oil
1/2 cup (125 ml) goat cheese

FOR PIRI-PIRI MAYONNAISE

1/4 cup (60 ml) mayonnaise
1 tsp piri-piri sauce

4 burger buns

PREPARATION

Brush red peppers with olive oil and place on a baking sheet. Roast for 5 minutes on each side or until skin is charred and easy to remove. Allow to cool in a covered bowl. Peel and seed cooled peppers, and then cut lengthwise into thin strips. Set aside.

Combine burger ingredients. Form 4 patties.

Cook patties for 5 to 6 minutes on each side.

Mix together mayonnaise and piri-piri sauce.

Toast buns. Spread piri-piri mayonnaise on bun bottoms and top with patties, goat cheese, and roasted red peppers. Serve.

BURGER WITH JACK SAUCE

SERVES 4

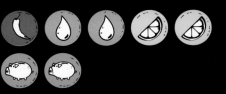

FOR WHISKEY BARBECUE SAUCE

1 onion, sliced
4 cloves garlic, sliced
1/2 cup (125 ml) whiskey (Jack Daniel's or bourbon of your choice)
2 cups (500 ml) ketchup
1/3 cup (80 ml) red wine vinegar
1/4 cup (60 ml) Worcestershire sauce
3/4 cup (180 ml) brown sugar
3/4 cup (180 ml) molasses
1/4 cup (60 ml) tomato paste
2 tsp liquid smoke
1 tsp salt
1 tsp ground pepper
1 tsp Tabasco sauce

4 burger buns

FOR BEEF BURGERS

1 lb ground beef
1 tbsp shallots or chives, finely chopped
2 tbsp ketchup
1 tbsp steak spice
1 egg
2 tbsp bread crumbs
Salt and freshly ground pepper

PREPARATION

In a pan, cook onion, garlic and whiskey for 10 minutes or until onion is softened. Add remaining sauce ingredients and cook for 20 minutes, stirring occasionally to prevent sauce from sticking. Strain with a mesh strainer.

Combine beef burger ingredients. Form 4 patties.

Cook patties for 5 to 6 minutes on each side.

Toast buns and top with patties and whisky barbecue sauce. Serve.

DID YOU KNOW?

This sauce keeps well in the refrigerator and its flavor only gets better with time!

PULLED PORK BURGER

SERVES 6

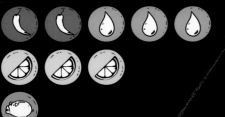

DID YOU KNOW?

Other countries have their own versions of pulled pork! Try Italian *porchetta*, French *rillettes*, or Mexican *carnitas*.

FOR PULLED PORK SEASONING

1 tbsp paprika
2 tbsp chili powder
1 tbsp garlic powder
1 tbsp dried mustard
1 tbsp thyme
1 tbsp liquid smoke
1/4 cup (60 ml) vegetable oil

FOR PULLED PORK

2 lbs pork shoulder
1 tbsp barbecue sauce

FOR CREAMY COLESLAW

2 cups green cabbage, very thinly sliced
1 small onion, very thinly sliced
1/2 cup (125 ml) mayonnaise
1/4 cup (60 ml) apple cider vinegar
1 tbsp sugar
1 tsp Worcestershire sauce
Salt and freshly ground pepper
1 carrot, grated

TOPPINGS

2 tbsp Dijon mustard
Sliced dill pickles

6 hamburger buns

PREPARATION

For pulled pork : Mix together seasoning ingredients. Rub pork shoulder with seasoning. Place in a roasting pan and cover with a lid or aluminum foil. Cook in a 300°F (150°C) for 4 hours.

Shred pork with two forks and add barbecue sauce.

For creamy coleslaw : Cook cabbage and onion in a large pot of boiling water for 10 seconds. Drain and chill.

In a bowl, whisk together mayonnaise, vinegar, sugar, Worcestershire, salt and pepper. Pour over cooked cabbage and onion, add grated carrot, and toss to coat. Refrigerate for at least 1 hour.

Toast buns. Spread Dijon mustard on bun bottoms. Top with pulled pork, coleslaw and pickles. Serve.

LAMB, PANCETTA & ROASTED GARLIC

SERVES 4

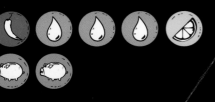

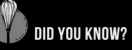

DID YOU KNOW?

Button mushrooms are cultivated in over 70 countries across the world.

FOR LAMB BURGERS

1 lb ground lamb
1 tbsp roasted garlic
1 tbsp fresh rosemary, chopped
1 egg
1 tbsp bread crumbs
1 tbsp steak spice

FOR ROASTED GARLIC

Olive oil
1 whole head garlic

FOR ROASTED GARLIC CHEESE SPREAD

1/4 cup (60 ml) goat cheese
1/4 cup (60 ml) cream cheese
1 tbsp roasted garlic
2 tbsp chives, chopped

TOPPINGS

16 button mushrooms
1 tbsp butter
Salt and freshly ground pepper
8 slices pancetta
4 slices tomato
2 tbsp Dijon mustard

4 English muffins

PREPARATION

For roasted garlic : Brush a baking sheet with olive oil. With a knife, cut off the top of a head of garlic, making sure the cloves don't separate. Place garlic cut side down on the oiled baking sheet and drizzle garlic head generously with olive oil. Roast in a 250°F (120°C) oven for 10 minutes; garlic should be golden brown but not charred. Remove from oven and let cool, and then squeeze out roasted garlic cloves. Purée in a food processor. In a jar or container, pour olive oil over garlic to cover. Store in the refrigerator.

For burger : Combine lamb burger ingredients. Form 4 patties and refrigerate.

In a bowl, mix together goat cheese, cream cheese, roasted garlic, and chives.

In a pan, sauté mushrooms in butter over high heat. Season with salt and pepper. Cook pancetta in a 350°F (175°C) for 10 minutes. Cook patties for 5 to 6 minutes on each side. Toast English muffins and top with patties, pancetta, mushrooms, tomato, and Dijon mustard.

PORK BURGERS WITH GREEN APPLE SLAW

SERVES 4

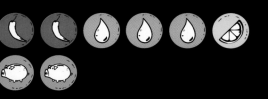

FOR PULLED PORK BURGER

2 cups (500 ml) pulled pork (see recipe on page 038)

FOR CARAMELIZED ONIONS

4 white onions, thinly sliced
2 tbsp butter
1 tbsp brown sugar
1/2 cup water
Salt and freshly ground pepper
1 tbsp sherry vinegar

FOR DIJONNAISE

2 tbsp mayonnaise
1 tbsp Dijon mustard

FOR APPLE SLAW

1 green apple, julienned
2 tbsp fresh parsley, chopped
1 tbsp olive oil
1 tbsp white wine vinegar

FOR GARNISH

4 slices cheddar cheese

4 burger buns

PREPARATION

Prepare pulled pork. (see recipe on page 038)

In a pan, brown onions in butter. Stir in sugar and cook until bottom of pan begins to brown, about 5 minutes. Add water and stir. Cover and cook for 5 minutes. Uncover and reduce until liquid has completely evaporated. Season with salt, pepper, and sherry vinegar. Set aside.

In a small bowl, combine mayonnaise and Dijon mustard. Set aside. In another bowl, mix together green apple, parsley, olive oil, and white wine vinegar. Set aside.

Toast buns. Spread mayonnaise on bun bottoms and top with pulled pork, apple slaw, caramelized onions, and cheddar cheese slices. Serve.

THE BARBARIAN

SERVES 4

FOR TARTARE

1 egg yolk
2 tbsp lemon juice
1 tbsp Dijon mustard
1 tbsp ketchup
1 tsp Worcestershire sauce
6 drops Tabasco sauce
1/4 cup (60 ml) olive oil
10 small sweet pickles, chopped
1/2 onion, finely chopped
2 tbsp parsley, chopped
1 lb beef tenderloin (or Boston cut),
finely chopped by hand with a sharp knife
Salt and freshly ground pepper

TOPPINGS

4 leaves lettuce (any kind)
4 slices tomato

4 burger buns (or country bread)

PREPARATION

In a bowl, whisk together egg yolk, lemon juice, mustard, ketchup, Worcestershire, and Tabasco for 2 minutes. Add oil in a steady stream, whisking vigorously until mixture becomes smooth. Add pickles, onion, parsley and meat. Mix well and season with salt and pepper. Set aside.

Toast buns and top with meat, lettuce and tomatoes. Serve.

DELUXE B.L.T.

SERVES 4

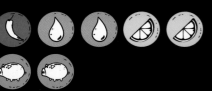

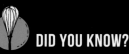 **DID YOU KNOW?**

eblochon is a soft washed-rind French cheese
 made with cow's milk. It is produced in the Alps
egions of Savoie and Haute-Savoie.

FOR VEAL BURGERS

1 lb ground veal
2 tbsp steak spice
2 tbsp bread crumbs
1 egg
2 tbsp ketchup
2 tbsp chives, chopped
Salt and freshly ground pepper

FOR TOMATO COMPOTE

1 can diced tomatoes, drained well
2 tbsp olive oil
1 small onion, finely chopped
2 cloves garlic, minced
1 tbsp dried oregano
1 tbsp chives, chopped
1 tbsp sugar
Salt and freshly ground pepper

TOPPINGS

1/2 pound reblochon cheese, rind removed
2 tbsp mayonnaise
8 slices bacon, cooked
A few leaves frisée lettuce

4 burger buns

PREPARATION

With a hand blender or in a food processor, roughly chop tomatoes with 1 tbsp olive oil. In a pan, heat remaining 1 tbsp olive oil and brown onions and garlic. In a bowl, combine cooked onions and garlic with tomatoes, oregano, chives, sugar, salt and pepper. Refrigerate.

In a bowl, combine veal burger ingredients. Form 4 patties and cook on the barbecue for 5 to 6 minutes on each side. Top each patty with reblochon cheese and allow cheese to melt.

Toast buns. Spread mayonnaise on bottom buns. Top with veal patties, bacon, tomato compote, and frisée lettuce. Serve.

9

THE CHIP SHOP BURGER

SERVES 4

TASTY TIP

Try this recipe with another white fish like haddock or cod!

FOR FISH BURGER

2 white fish (turbot) fillets, cut in half
Salt and freshly ground pepper
1/2 cup (125 ml) flour
2 eggs, beaten
1/2 cup (125 ml) bread crumbs
1/4 cup (60 ml) vegetable oil

FOR TARTAR SAUCE

1 cup (250 ml) mayonnaise
2 tbsp Dijon mustard
1 dill pickle, chopped
2 tbsp capers, chopped
2 tbsp chives, chopped
1 shallot, minced
Freshly ground pepper

FOR GREEN PEA PURÉE

1 cup (250 ml) green peas
10 fresh mint leaves
Juice of 1/2 lemon
2 tbsp olive oil
Salt and freshly ground pepper

FOR GARNISH

4 lemon wedges

4 burger buns

PREPARATION

In a small bowl, combine tartar sauce ingredients. Set aside.

With a hand blender or in a food processor, purée green peas, mint, lemon juice, oil, and salt and pepper. Add water as needed.

Season fish with salt and pepper. Dredge in flour, dip in egg, and coat with bread crumbs. In a pan, heat oil and fry fish for 2 to 3 minutes on each side until golden brown. Set aside.

Toast buns. Spread tartar sauce on bottom buns and top with fried fish and green pea purée. Serve with lemon wedges on the side.

THE BACON SURPRISE

SERVES 4

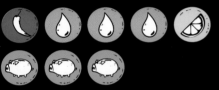

FOR BEEF BURGERS

1 lb ground beef
1 egg
1 tbsp steak spice
2 tbsp bread crumbs
1 tbsp ketchup
2 tbsp shallots or chives, finely chopped

FOR BACON FILLING

6 slices bacon, finely chopped
1 onion, finely chopped
4 slices sharp cheddar, cut into small cubes

4 burger buns

PREPARATION

In a pan, fry onion and bacon. Allow to cool slightly and then stir in cheese. Set aside.

In a bowl, combine burger ingredients. Divide mixture into 8 equal portions and form into patties. To stuff burgers, sandwich a spoonful of the onion, bacon and cheese mixture between two patties, seal the edges, and repeat with remaining patties. Cook for 5 to 6 minutes on each side.

Toast buns and top with stuffed burgers and your favorite condiments.

 **DID YOU KNOW?**

Cheddar is a hard, pale to deep yellow, typically sharp-tasting cheese that originated in the village of Cheddar in Somerset, England.

PROSCIUTTO TILAPIA BUNDLES

SERVES 4

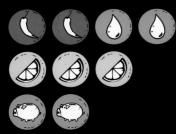

FOR CHIMICHURRI SAUCE

1 1/2 cups fresh parsley with stems
3 cloves garlic
1/4 cup (60 ml) fresh oregano
1 tsp paprika
1/2 cup (125 ml) olive oil
2 tbsp red (or white) wine vinegar
Salt and freshly ground pepper
1 tsp crushed red pepper flakes

FOR TILAPIA PROSCIUTTO BUNDLES

8 slices prosciutto
2 tilapia fillets, cut in half
1 tbsp vegetable oil

FOR GARNISH TOPPINGS

2 tbsp mayonnaise
8 cherry tomatoes, quartered

4 burger buns

PREPARATION

With a hand blender or in a food processor, purée chimichurri ingredients until smooth. Let sit for 30 minutes.

Make an X with 2 prosciutto slices and place a piece of tilapia in the middle. Wrap prosciutto around tilapia. Repeat with remaining prosciutto slices and tilapia. Place bundles on a tray brushed with vegetable oil. Fillets should be sitting on prosciutto ends to keep meat tightly wrapped around each piece. Cook in a 350°F (180°C) oven for 15 minutes.

Toast buns. Spread mayonnaise on bottom buns and top with tilapia prosciutto bundles. Garnish with tomatoes and chimichurri sauce and serve.

 **DID YOU KNOW?**

Chimichurri is a popular South American green sauce similar to salsa verde, typically used for grilled meats.

AL PASTOR BURGER

SERVES 4

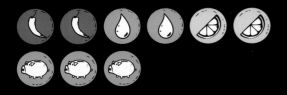

 **DID YOU KNOW?**

Widely cultivated in Mexico, the guajillo chili is a long, slightly curved pepper with deep orange-red flesh. It has a mild green tea flavor with berry overtones and only a small amount of heat.

FOR PORK AND PINEAPPLE

1 lb pork loin, thinly sliced
2 cups (500 ml) fresh pineapple, cubed
1 tbsp vegetable oil

FOR AL PASTOR MARINADE

1 onion
1/2 cup (125 ml) orange juice
1/4 cup (60 ml) white wine vinegar
3 guajillo chili peppers, cut in half and seeded
2 cloves garlic
1 tbsp ground cumin

TOPPINGS

1 onion, chopped
1 cup (250 ml) fresh cilantro leaves

FOR GARNISH

4 lime wedges

4 burger buns

PREPARATION

With a hand blender or in a food processor, purée onion, orange juice, white wine vinegar, guajillo peppers, garlic, and cumin. In a pan, cook mixture for 15 minutes. Refrigerate. When marinade is cool, pour over sliced pork and pineapple. Marinate in the refrigerator for at least 5 hours.

Remove pork and pineapple from marinade. In a pan, heat vegetable oil and sear pork and pineapple for 1 to 2 minutes.

Toast buns in the oven. Top with pork and pineapples, chopped onions, and fresh cilantro. Finish with a squeeze of lemon and serve.

CRISPY CHICKEN CRUNCHBURGER

SERVES 4

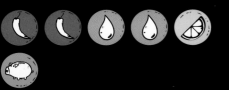

DID YOU KNOW?

Harissa is a fiery Tunisian pepper sauce often used in couscous or with olive oil as a dipping sauce for bread. The name comes from the Arabic word *harasa*, which means to pound or break into pieces.

FOR MARINADE

1 onion, chopped
1 tsp paprika
1 tsp Harissa
Juice of 1/2 lemon
2 cloves garlic, crushed
1 chicken bouillon cube, crumbled
Leaves from 2 sprigs fresh thyme
Freshly ground pepper

FOR FRIED CHICKEN

4 boneless skinless chicken thighs
1/2 cup (125 ml) bread crumbs
2 tbsp fresh Parmesan cheese, grated
1/2 cup (125 ml) flour
2 eggs, beaten
2 tbsp vegetable oil

FOR GARNISH

2 tbsp mayonnaise
1 tomato, sliced
A few leaves lettuce (any kind)

4 burger buns

PREPARATION

Combine marinade ingredients. Coat chicken in mixture and marinate overnight.

In a bowl, mix together bread crumbs and Parmesan cheese. When the chicken has finished marinating, dredge in flour, dip in egg, and coat with bread crumbs. In a pan, heat oil and fry chicken on each side. Transfer to a baking sheet and cook in a 350°F (175°C) oven for 10 minutes.

Toast buns. Spread mayonnaise on bottom buns and top with fried chicken thighs, tomato slices, and lettuce. Serve.

14

CAJUN SHRIMP BURGER

SERVES 4

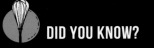
DID YOU KNOW?

The stigmas (or threads) of the saffron flower are painstakingly collected by hand, which is why it's the most expensive spice in the world. Because each flower only bears three stigmas, it takes 150,000 flowers to produce 2.2 pounds of fresh saffron and almost 11 pounds of fresh saffron to produce 2.2 pounds of dried saffron!

FOR SHRIMP

2 tbsp olive oil
1 shallot, minced
1 yellow pepper, cut into thin strips
1 clove garlic, minced
20 small raw shrimp, peeled
Juice of 1 lime

FOR CAJUN SEASONING

1 tsp dried thyme
1 tsp paprika
1 tsp brown sugar, packed
1 tsp ground cumin
1/2 tsp dried mustard
1/2 tsp crushed red pepper flakes
1/2 tsp salt

FOR SAFFRON MAYONNAISE

1 pinch Spanish saffron
2 tbsp hot water
1/4 cup (60 ml) mayonnaise
Zest of 1/2 lime

TOPPINGS

A few leaves iceberg lettuce

4 burger buns

PREPARATION

Infuse saffron in hot water. Allow to cool. Combine saffron infusion, mayonnaise, and lime zest. Refrigerate for 30 minutes.

In a small bowl, mix together Cajun seasoning ingredients. Set aside.

In a pan, heat olive oil over medium heat and cook shallot and yellow pepper until softened. Add garlic, shrimp, and Cajun seasoning. Cook for 3 to 4 minutes and then add lime juice.

Toast buns. Spread saffron mayonnaise on bun bottoms and top with Cajun shrimp and lettuce. Serve.

15

TOTAL TOFU

SERVES 4

FOR TOFU BURGERS

1 tbsp olive oil
1/2 red onion, minced
10 button mushrooms, sliced
2 cloves garlic, finely
1 tbsp tomato paste
1 cup (250 ml) cilantro, chopped
1 1/2 cups (375 ml) firm tofu
2 tbsp balsamic vinegar
2 tbsp chili sauce
250 ml (1 cup) whole wheat bread crumbs

TOPPINGS

1 tbsp cream cheese
8 sundried tomatoes in oil
1 handful baby spinach

4 burger buns

PREPARATION

In a pan, heat olive oil and cook onion until golden brown. Add mushrooms and garlic and cook for 2 minutes. Stir in tomato paste. Set aside.

With a hand blender or in a food processor, purée cilantro, tofu, balsamic vinegar, and chili sauce until smooth.

In a bowl, combine mushroom mixture and tofu mixture.

Form into 4 patties, coat with bread crumbs, and cook for 3 or 4 minutes on each side in a hot, oiled pan.

Toast buns. Spread cream cheese on bun bottoms and top with tofu patties, sundried tomatoes, and spinach. Serve.

THE JAMAICAN

SERVES 4

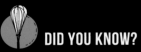

DID YOU KNOW?

The habañero (scotch bonnet) pepper is an EXTREMELY hot chili with a smoky, fruity flavor and yellow, orange or red flesh. These peppers are cultivated in Jamaica, Belize, and the Caribbean islands, and are the one of the staples of Jamaican cuisine.

4 boneless skinless chicken thighs

FOR JAMAICAN MARINADE

2 tsp allspice
1/2 tsp ground nutmeg
1/2 tsp ground mace
1 tsp salt
1 tbsp brown sugar
2 tsp thyme
1 tsp black pepper
1 1/2 cups (375 ml) green onions, thinly sliced
1 habañero (scotch bonnet) pepper
2 cloves garlic
2 tbsp vegetable oil

FOR COLESLAW

2 cups (500 ml) green cabbage, very thinly sliced
1/2 red onion, very thinly sliced
2 tbsp fresh thyme, chopped
1/4 cup (60 ml) mayonnaise
1/4 cup (60 ml) orange juice
Salt and freshly ground pepper

TOPPINGS

2 tbsp mayonnaise

4 hamburger buns

PREPARATION

With a hand blender or in a food processor, purée marinade ingredients until smooth. Brush chicken thighs with mixture and refrigerate for at least 4 hours.

In a bowl, combine coleslaw ingredients. Refrigerate for 2 hours.

Cook chicken on the barbecue for 5 to 7 minutes on each side.

Toast buns. Spread mayonnaise on bun bottoms and top with chicken thighs and coleslaw. Serve.

17

VEGGIE PORTOBELLO BURGER

SERVES 4

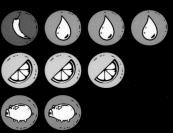

FOR BALSAMIC MARINADE

2 sprigs fresh rosemary, leaves removed from stems
1 tbsp Dijon mustard
2 cloves garlic, minced
1/2 cup (125 ml) olive oil
1/2 cup (125 ml) balsamic vinegar

FOR MARINATED VEGETABLES

4 portobello mushrooms caps
8 slices roasted red peppers
(store-bought marinated in oil or see recipe on page 034)
4 slices eggplant
1 zucchini, thinly sliced
1 red onion, sliced into rounds

TOPPINGS

4 slices goat cheese with rind
1 handful arugula
2 tbsp basil pesto

4 burger buns

PREPARATION

In a bowl, mix together marinade ingredients. Pour 2 tbsp marinade into each portobello mushroom hollow and combine remaining marinade with roasted red pepper slices, eggplant, zucchini and onion. Let marinate for 1 hour.

Cook marinated portobellos and vegetables on the barbecue or in a 350°F (175°C) oven for 15 minutes. Top each cap with a slice of goat cheese and cook until mushrooms are tender.

Toast buns. Spread pesto on bun bottoms and top with cheesy portobellos, a few grilled vegetables, and arugula. Serve.

DID YOU KNOW?

Portobello burgers are perfect for committed carnivores who want to eat more veggies—the mushrooms have a chewy, meaty texture and a rich, earthy flavor.

18

GARLIC BUTTER EXPLOSION

SERVES 4

DID YOU KNOW?

To freshen breath after eating garlicky food, just munch on a bit of parsley or mint!

FOR GARLIC BUTTER

1/2 cup (125 ml) butter, slightly softened
2 cloves garlic, minced
1 pinch parsley, very finely chopped
1 tbsp lemon juice
Freshly ground pepper

FOR BURGERS

1 lb ground beef
2 tbsp shallots, finely chopped
2 tbsp bread crumbs
1 egg
2 tbsp ketchup
1 tbsp steak spice

TOPPINGS

Choice of condiments

4 hamburger buns

PREPARATION

In a pan, heat 1 tbsp butter and cook garlic until golden. Combine with remaining softened butter, parsley, lemon juice, and pepper to taste. Form garlic butter into a log about 1 inch in diameter and put in the freezer.

In a bowl, combine burger ingredients. Form into 4 patties and set aside.

Once the butter has hardened, slice into 1/4-inch rounds. Insert one round into the center of each patty and seal to ensure that the butter is fully covered. Cook patties for 6 to 8 minutes on each side.

Toast buns and top with patties and your favorite condiments. Serve.

BREAKFAST BURGER

SERVES 4

FOR BURGERS

Meat from 4 breakfast sausages
2 tbsp vegetable oil

TOPPINGS

4 slices cheddar cheese
6 slices bacon, cooked
4 eggs
Salt and freshly ground pepper
1 tbsp butter
2 tbsp mayonnaise
4 tomato slices

4 English muffins

PREPARATION

Form 4 patties with sausage meat. In a pan, heat vegetable oil and cook patties for about 3 minutes on each side. Top with cheddar cheese and bacon. Keep warm.

In a small bowl, beat eggs and season with salt and pepper.

In a non-stick pan, heat butter. Add eggs and cook for 2 minutes. Divide eggs into 4 equal portions and flip to finish cooking.

Toast English muffins. Spread mayonnaise on bottom halves of muffins and top with sausage patties, eggs, and tomato slices. Serve.

THE COFFEE COWBOY

SERVES 4

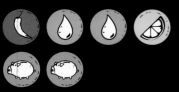

FOR BURGERS

1 lb ground beef

FOR COFFEE RUB

1 tbsp ground coffee
3 tbsp brown sugar
2 tsp crushed black pepper
1/2 tsp ground coriander
1/2 tsp dried oregano
1/2 tsp salt

FOR ROASTED ONIONS WITH THYME AND GARLIC

2 white onions, sliced into rounds
4 sprigs fresh thyme
2 cloves garlic, roughly chopped
2 tbsp butter
Salt and freshly ground pepper

TOPPINGS

4 slices smoked cheese (gouda)
2 tbsp store-bought barbecue sauce

4 burger buns

PREPARATION

Evenly spread onions, thyme and garlic on a baking sheet. Distribute small pieces of butter over the mixture, season with salt and pepper, and cook in a 500°F (260°C) oven for 10 minutes or until onions are golden brown. Set aside.

In a bowl, combine coffee rub ingredients. Form 4 patties. Rub each patty with 1 tbsp coffee rub. Cook for 5 to 6 minutes each side. Top with cheese slices and allow cheese to melt.

Toast buns. Spread barbecue sauce on bun bottoms and top with patties and onion mixture. Serve.

TASTY TIP

Instead of plain hamburger buns, try hearty grain bread, French baguette, or chewy *ciabatta*!

THE AUSTRALIAN

SERVES 4

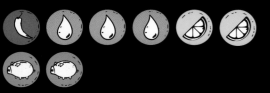

FOR BEEF BURGERS

1 lb ground beef
1 tbsp steak spice
2 tbsp bread crumbs
2 tbsp shallots or chives, minced
2 tbsp ketchup
1 egg

TOPPINGS

4 slices cheddar cheese
8 slices pickled beets
8 slices bacon, cooked
4 slices tomato
1 small onion, sliced into rounds
A few leaves iceberg lettuce
4 eggs, cooked sunny-side up

4 burger buns

PREPARATION

In a bowl, combine burger ingredients. Form 4 patties.

Cook patties for 5 to 6 minutes on each side. Top with cheddar cheese and allow cheese to melt.

Toast buns and top with patties, pickled beets, bacon, tomato and onion slices, lettuce, and sunny-side up eggs. Serve.

TASTY TIP

Add even more toppings to make it a truly authentic Australian burger!

22

VEGGIE BLACK BEAN BURGER

SERVES 4

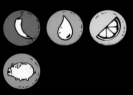

FOR BLACK BEAN BURGERS

4 tbsp vegetable oil
1 new potato, peeled and cut into small cubes
1 onion, finely chopped
2 cloves garlic, minced
1 tsp cumin
1/4 cup (60 ml) shiitake mushrooms,
rehydrated and finely chopped
Salt and freshly ground pepper
1 1/2 cups (375 ml) canned black beans, drained and rinsed
1 tsp smoked paprika
1/4 cup (60 ml) Parmesan cheese, grated
Juice of 1 lemon
1/4 cup (60 ml) bread crumbs
1 egg

TOPPINGS

2 tbsp mayonnaise
Choice of condiments

4 burger buns

PREPARATION

In a pan, heat 2 tbsp vegetable oil and fry cubed potato for 5 minutes. Add onion, garlic, cumin, and shiitake mushrooms and cook until potato cubes are easily pierced with a knife. Season with salt and pepper and let cool.

In a bowl, combine cooled potato mixture with black beans, smoked paprika, Parmesan cheese, lemon juice, bread crumbs, and egg. Mix together with your hands and form 4 patties.

In a non-stick pan, heat remaining 2 tbsp vegetable oil and fry patties for 5 minutes on each side.

Toast buns. Spread mayonnaise on bun bottoms and top with patties and condiments. Serve.

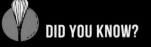

DID YOU KNOW?

Shiitake mushrooms have been grown in Japan, China and Korea since prehistoric times. They can be used fresh and dried and are a source of antioxidants.

23

THE
SLOPPY JOE

SERVES 4

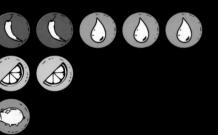

TASTY TIP

...o all out by adding a few slices of cheese to your ...loppy joes!

DID YOU KNOW?

...egend has it the original sloppy joe was ...vented in the 1930s by a cook named Joe in ...ioux City, Iowa. Today, almost every state has ...s own version of the classic American sandwich!

FOR SLOPPY JOE FILLING

1 tbsp vegetable oil
1 onion, finely chopped
1 green pepper, cut into small dice
2 cloves garlic, minced
1 lb lean ground beef
Salt and freshly ground pepper
3/4 cup (180 ml) tomato sauce
1 tbsp tomato paste
1/2 cup (125 ml) store-bought barbecue sauce
(or see recipe on page 036)
1 tsp Worcestershire sauce
2 tsp paprika
6 drops Tabasco sauce

4 burger buns

PREPARATION

In a large pan, heat oil and cook onion, pepper and garlic until softened. Add ground beef and brown. Season with salt and pepper and add remaining ingredients. Simmer for 10 minutes until sauce is thick.

Toast buns and top with sloppy joe mixture.

CHICKEN SOUVLAKI BURGER

SERVES 4

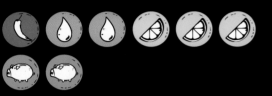

TASTY TIP

Add some slices of fresh feta cheese!

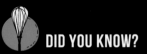
DID YOU KNOW?

Ras el hanout means "top of the shop" in Arabic and refers to a blend of the best spices a seller has to offer. This spice mixture is popular in Morocco and across North Africa.

FOR CHICKEN BURGERS

2 chicken breasts, cut in half
1/4 cup (60 ml) tzatziki
2 tbsp Ras el hanout
Juice of 1/2 lemon

FOR CUCUMBER SALAD

1 cucumber, thinly sliced into rounds
2 tbsp fresh mint, chopped
2 tbsp olive oil
1 tsp sherry vinegar

TOPPINGS

1/2 cup (125 ml) tzatziki
1 tsp Ras el hanout
4 slices tomato

4 burger buns

PREPARATION

In a bowl, combine tzatziki sauce, Ras el hanout, and lemon juice. Marinate chicken in mixture for at least 4 hours.

In a salad bowl, mix together salad ingredients. Set aside.

Combine tzatziki sauce and Ras el hanout. Set aside.

When chicken has finished marinating, cook for 6 to 8 minutes on each side or until fully cooked through.

Toast buns. Spread tzatziki sauce on bun bottoms and top with grilled chicken, tomato slices, and cucumber salad. Serve.

25

WELSH RAREBIT BURGER

SERVES 4

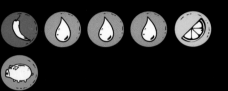

TASTY TIP

Serve your burgers with a scrumptious salad from *The World's 60 Best Salads… Period!*

DID YOU KNOW?

Welsh rarebit (or Welsh rabbit) is a traditional English dish made with toast and a creamy, cheesy beer sauce. It has been a staple of British cuisine for over 300 years!

FOR PORK AND HAM BURGERS

1/2 pound ground pork
1/2 pound cooked, smoked or cured ham, chopped by hand or in a food processor
1 tbsp Dijon mustard
Salt and freshly ground pepper
2 tbsp bread crumbs

1 egg

FOR WELSH RAREBIT SAUCE

1 tbsp butter
1 tbsp flour
1 bottle pale or amber beer
2 cups (500 ml) sharp cheddar cheese, grated
Salt and freshly ground pepper

4 burger buns

PREPARATION

To prepare Welsh sauce, melt butter in a small pot. Add flour and cook for 1 minute. Gradually add beer, whisking constantly, until sauce thickens. Remove from heat and stir in cheese. Season with salt and pepper. Keep warm.

Combine burger ingredients. Form 4 patties.

Cook patties for 6 to 7 minutes on each side.

Toast buns and top with patties. Pour a generous spoonful of Welsh rarebit sauce over each burger and serve.

26

MINI CRAB CAKE BURGER

12 UNITÉS

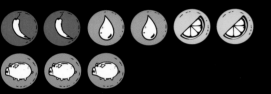

FOR CRAB CAKES

1/2 pound crab meat
1 store-bought roasted red pepper (or see recipe on page 034)
1 tbsp mayonnaise
1 tbsp green onions, thinly sliced
1/4 cup (60 ml) Japanese bread crumbs (panko)
1 egg
1/4 cup (60 ml) corn
1 tsp smoked paprika
1 tbsp cumin
1 squeeze of lemon juice
4 drops Tabasco sauce
Salt and freshly ground pepper

FOR BREAD CRUMB COATING

1 tbsp flour
2 eggs, beaten
1 cup (250 ml) Japanese bread crumbs (panko)
3 tbsp vegetable oil

FOR CUMIN MAYONNAISE

3 tbsp mayonnaise
1 tbsp wholegrain mustard
1 tsp cumin
Juice of 1/2 lemon

TOPPINGS

6 cherry tomatoes, halved
12 mini burger buns

PREPARATION

In a small bowl, mix together mayonnaise, wholegrain mustard, cumin and lemon juice. Refrigerate.

In a large bowl, combine crab cake ingredients. Add more bread crumbs if mixture is too dry. Chill for 15 minutes. Form 12 small patties, dredge in flour, dip in egg, and coat with bread crumbs. In a pan or a deep fryer, fry crab patties in vegetable oil. Set aside.

Toast buns. Spread mayonnaise on bun bottoms and top with crab cakes and tomatoes. Serve.

DID YOU KNOW?

Panko is a variety of Japanese bread crumb made from crustless bread. When fried, it has a crunchier, airier texture than traditional bread crumbs.

PORK, ZUCCHINI & JALAPEÑO

SERVES 4

FOR PORK BURGERS

1 lb ground pork
2 tbsp steak spice
1 dash Worcestershire sauce
2 tbsp bread crumbs
1/4 cup parsley, chopped
1 egg

FOR JALAPEÑO SOUR CREAM

1 tbsp olive oil
1 onion, finely chopped
2 jalapeño peppers, seeded and minced
1/4 cup (60 ml) sour cream
Zest of 1 lime
Salt and freshly ground pepper

TOPPINGS

1 tbsp olive oil
2 zucchinis, sliced lengthwise
4 slices Monterey jack cheese

4 burger buns

PREPARATION

In a bowl, combine pork burger ingredients. Form into 4 patties and refrigerate.

In a pan, heat 1 tbsp olive oil and brown onion and jalapeño peppers. Allow to cool, and then combine with sour cream and lime zest. Season generously with salt and freshly ground pepper.

Brush zucchini slices with 1 tbsp olive oil and grill.

Cook patties for 5 to 6 minutes on each side. Top with Monterey jack slices and allow cheese to melt.

Toast buns. Spread jalapeño sour cream on bun bottoms and top with patties and grilled zucchini. Serve.

THE OKTOBERFEST

SERVES 4

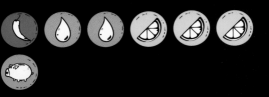

DID YOU KNOW?

The smallest beer you can buy at *Oktoberfest* is a *Maßkrug*—that's a one liter mug of beer!

TASTY TIP

Serve with beer and a side of pickles!

FOR SAUSAGE PATTIES

1 onion, finely chopped
Meat from 3 mild sausages (any kind)
1 tbsp Dijon mustard
1 beer (any kind)

TOPPINGS

1 tbsp wholegrain mustard
1 cup (250 ml) sauerkraut in white wine
4 slices emmental cheese

4 burger buns

PREPARATION

In a pan, cook onion until softened. Add sausage meat and Dijon mustard and cook for a few minutes. Remove from heat and form into 4 patties. Place patties side by side in a casserole dish with a flat bottom and pour beer over meat. Marinate in the refrigerator for 1 hour.

Cook patties on the barbecue for 5 to 6 minutes on each side. Top with emmental cheese slices and allow cheese to melt.

Toast buns. Spread wholegrain mustard on bun bottoms and top with patties, sauerkraut and more mustard. Serve.

MERMAID CROQUETTE

SERVES 4

FOR FISH CROQUETTES

1 new potato, peeled and chopped
1 lb white fish (cod), cut into large cubes
2 tbsp mayonnaise
1 stalk celery, cut into a small dice
1 shallot, minced
1 egg
1/4 cup (60 ml) bread crumbs
2 tbsp fresh tarragon, chopped
6 drops Tabasco sauce
1/4 cup (60 ml) flour
1 tbsp vegetable oil

FOR HARISSA MAYONNAISE

1/4 cup (60 ml) mayonnaise
Zest and juice of 1 lime
1 tsp harissa sauce

TOPPINGS

1 handful arugula

4 burger buns

PREPARATION

In a small bowl, combine mayonnaise, lime zest and juice, and harissa. Refrigerate.

Fill a pot with cold water. Add potato and bring to a boil. When potato is cooked, add fish and simmer for 5 minutes. Drain and allow to cool. Add remaining fish croquette ingredients except vegetable oil and mix together with your hands. Form 4 patties and dredge in flour. Set aside.

In a pan, heat vegetable oil and cook croquettes for 3 to 4 minutes on each side until golden brown.

Toast buns. Spread mayonnaise on bun bottoms and top with fish croquettes and a few arugula leaves. Serve.

TASTY TIP

Try this recipe with tilapia or sole!

PORK & SHRIMP WITH PINEAPPLE SALSA

SERVES 4

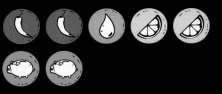

FOR PORK AND SHRIMP BURGERS

1 egg
2 tbsp soy sauce
1 tbsp sesame oil
1 tbsp fresh ginger, finely grated
1 clove garlic, minced
1/2 pound medium raw shrimp, peeled and finely chopped
1/2 pound ground pork
2 green onions, thinly sliced
1 tsp vegetable oil
Salt and freshly ground pepper
1/4 cup (60 ml) bread crumbs

FOR PINEAPPLE SALSA

1 tbsp olive oil
2 slices bacon, diced
1/2 red pepper, finely chopped
1 shallot, minced
2 tbsp cilantro, chopped
1 tsp lemon juice
1/2 cup pineapple, chopped
A few drops Tabasco sauce
Salt and freshly ground pepper

TOPPINGS

Mayonnaise to taste

4 burger buns

PREPARATION

In a bowl, combine burger ingredients. Form into 4 patties. Set aside.

In a pan, heat olive oil and cook bacon, red pepper, and shallot for 5 minutes. Remove from heat and add cilantro, lemon juice, chopped pineapple, and Tabasco sauce, and season with salt and pepper. Set aside.

Cook patties for 5 to 6 minutes on each side.

Toast buns. Spread mayonnaise on bun bottoms and top with pork and shrimp burgers and pineapple salsa. Serve.

TASTY TIP

If you're not a fan of pineapple, use mango instead!

CHICKEN PARMESAN

SERVES 4

FOR CHICKEN

2 chicken breasts, cut in half
Salt and freshly ground pepper
1/2 cup (125 ml) flour
2 eggs, beaten
1/2 cup (125 ml) Italian bread crumbs
2 tbsp vegetable oil
1/2 cup (125 ml) homemade or store-bought tomato sauce
1/4 cup (60 ml) fresh oregano
1/4 cup (60 ml) Parmesan cheese, grated

FOR GARLIC BUTTER

1/4 cup (60 ml) butter, softened
2 cloves garlic, minced
1 tsp lemon juice
Freshly ground pepper

TOPPINGS

1 cup (250 ml) mozzarella cheese, grated

4 burger buns

PREPARATION

In a pan, cook garlic in 1 tbsp butter. In a small bowl, combine remaining butter with garlic, lemon juice, and freshly ground pepper and stir until smooth. Set aside.

Place chicken between 2 pieces of plastic wrap and flatten with a mallet until pieces are about 1/2-inch thick. Season with salt and pepper and then dredge in flour, dip in egg, and coat with bread crumbs.

In an oven-safe skillet, heat vegetable oil and sear chicken until exterior is golden brown. Cover with tomato sauce, oregano, and Parmesan cheese and bake in a 350°F (180°C) oven for 10 minutes.

Cut buns and spread garlic butter on top and bottom buns. Sprinkle with grated mozzarella and broil in the oven until golden. Top with baked chicken and serve.

SALMON CILANTRO BURGER

SERVES 4

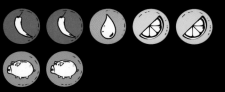

DID YOU KNOW?

Cilantro helps to improve digestion.

FOR SALMON BURGERS

1 lb salmon, chopped into small pieces
2 jalapeño peppers, seeded and minced
2 shallots, minced
1/4 cup (60 ml) cilantro, chopped
Zest of 1 lime
Salt and freshly ground pepper
2 egg whites
1/4 cup (60 ml) flour
2 tbsp vegetable oil

FOR LIME MAYONNAISE

1/4 cup (60 ml) mayonnaise
Zest and juice of 1 lime
Freshly ground pepper

TOPPINGS

1 handful baby spinach leaves
4 slices feta cheese

4 burger buns

PREPARATION

In a small bowl, combine mayonnaise, lime zest and juice, and pepper. Refrigerate.

In a bowl, mix together salmon, jalapeños, shallots, cilantro, lime zest, and salt and pepper. Set aside.

In a small bowl, beat egg whites until stiff and then gently fold in chopped salmon. Gradually sprinkle in flour to prevent lumps from forming. Refrigerate for 30 minutes.

Form 4 patties with salmon mixture. In a very hot non-stick pan, heat oil. Cook patties until a golden crust has formed and then flip and cook for another 3 to 4 minutes.

Toast buns. Spread mayonnaise on bun bottoms and top with salmon patties, baby spinach leaves, and feta cheese slices. Serve.

DUCK, HAZELNUT & MANGO

SERVES 4

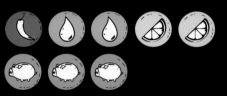

FOR DUCK BURGERS

1 tbsp olive oil
1 red onion, finely chopped
1 clove garlic, minced
2 confit duck legs, meat removed and shredded
1/4 cup (60 ml) hazelnuts, roughly chopped
1/4 cup (60 ml) red wine
2 tbsp honey
1 tbsp sherry vinegar

FOR MANGO MAYONNAISE

3 tbsp mayonnaise
2 tbsp store-bought mango chutney

TOPPINGS

1 green apple, thinly sliced
1 celery stalk, cut lengthwise into thin slices
1 handful mesclun or arugula

4 burger buns

PREPARATION

In a pan, cook onion and garlic in olive oil. Add duck, hazelnuts, red wine, honey and vinegar. Allow the mixture to reduce until duck is coated in a thick sauce.

Mix together mayonnaise and mango chutney.

Toast buns. Spread mango mayonnaise on bun bottoms and top with duck, apple slices, celery and mesclun. Serve.

THE FOUR CHEESE BURGER

SERVES 4

FOR BEEF BURGERS

1 lb ground beef
1 clove garlic, minced
1 shallot or a few chives, finely chopped
1 tbsp Worcestershire sauce
1 tbsp ketchup
1 tbsp Parmesan cheese, grated
Salt and freshly ground pepper

TOPPINGS

4 slices orange cheddar
4 slices Swiss cheese
4 slices goat cheese with rind
4 large slices tomato
4 tbsp Parmesan cheese, grated
1 handful arugula

4 burger buns

PREPARATION

Combine beef burger ingredients. Form 4 patties.

Cook patties for 5 minutes on one side. Flip and top each patty with a slice of cheddar, a slice of goat cheese, a slice of tomato, a slice of Swiss cheese, and grated Parmesan. Continue to cook for 5 to 6 minutes.

Toast buns and top with arugula and cheese-smothered patties.

 **DID YOU KNOW?**

Arugula has a high concentration of vitamin K, which helps prevent cardiovascular problems and osteoperosis.

LAMB, BACON & BLUE CHEESE SAUCE

SERVES 4

FOR BLUE CHEESE SAUCE

1 tbsp butter
1/2 small onion, finely chopped
1 tbsp flour
1 cup (250 ml) milk
1/2 cup (125 ml) blue cheese, crumbled
1 pinch cayenne pepper
2 tbsp chives, chopped
Salt and freshly ground pepper

FOR LAMB BURGERS

1 lb ground lamb
2 tbsp steak spice
2 tbsp ketchup
1 egg
2 tbsp bread crumbs
2 tbsp shallots or chives, finely chopped

TOPPINGS

6 slices bacon, cooked
1 bag plain potato chips

4 burger buns

PREPARATION

In a small pot, melt butter and cook onion until softened. Add flour and cook for 1 minute. Gradually add milk, whisking constantly until sauce becomes thick. Remove from heat and stir in blue cheese, cayenne pepper, and chives. Season with salt and pepper and set aside.

Combine lamb burger ingredients and form 4 patties. Cook for 5 to 6 minutes on each side.

Toast buns. Top with patties and bacon. Smother each burger with sauce and garnish with a few chips, or serve chips on the side with a small bowl of blue cheese sauce for dipping.

36

THE ROSSINI BURGER

SERVES 4

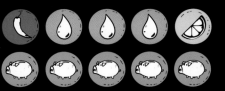

DID YOU KNOW?

Truffles—the Italian white truffle in particular—are the most expensive mushrooms in the world. Rich, oily foods like charcuterie and foie gras bring out their complex aroma, and usually just a few thin shavings are needed to add unique depth to a dish.

FOR BEEF BURGERS

1 lb lean ground beef
2 tbsp steak spice
Salt and pepper

FOR MADEIRA DEMI-GLACE SAUCE

1/4 cup (60 ml) Madeira wine or white port
2 cups (500 ml) store-bought veal demi-glace
1 tbsp truffle paste
1/2 tsp sherry vinegar
1 tbsp butter
Salt and freshly ground pepper

TOPPINGS

4 slices foie gras (about 1/2-inch thick each)
A few slices fresh truffle (optional)

4 burger buns

PREPARATION

Season beef with steak spice, salt and pepper. Form 4 patties. Cook in a large pan for 5 to 6 minutes on each side. Remove burgers from pan and keep warm.

Deglaze pan with Madeira. Add demi-glace, truffle paste, and sherry vinegar, and reduce until sauce is smooth and thick enough to coat the back of a spoon. Whisk in butter and season with salt and pepper. Put patties back into pan and thoroughly coat with sauce.

In another, unoiled pan, sear foie gras over very high heat for 10 seconds on each side.

Toast buns. Top with patties and foie gras. Spoon 1 tbsp sauce over each burger, garnish with fresh truffle slices, and serve.

LAMB PITA BABA

SERVES 4

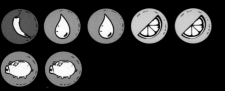

FOR LAMB BURGERS

1 lb ground lamb
3 tbsp 35% cream
1 carrot, finely grated
2 tbsp garam masala
1 onion, finely chopped
1/4 cup (60 ml) sliced almonds
2 tbsp bread crumbs
1 egg
Salt and freshly ground pepper

TOPPINGS

1/4 cup (60 ml) fresh sheep's milk cheese
4 slices tomato
1/4 cup (60 ml) store-bought baba ghanoush

4 Lebanese-style pitas

PREPARATION

Combine lamb burger ingredients. Form 4 fairly thin patties. Cut out 2 patty-sized circles from each pita to use as buns. Cook patties for 5 to 6 minutes on each side.

Toast buns. Spread cheese on bun bottoms. Top with patties, tomatoes and baba ghanoush.

 **DID YOU KNOW?**

Baba ghanoush is a popular Middle Eastern side dish made with roasted eggplant, olive oil, and various seasonings.

MINI BLUEBERRY COCKTAIL BURGER

MAKES 12 MINI BURGERS

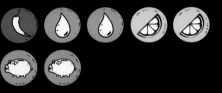

FOR LAMB BURGERS

1 lb ground lamb
1 tbsp allspice
2 tbsp bread crumbs
1 egg
Salt and freshly ground pepper

FOR BLUEBERRY CHUTNEY

2 cups (500 ml) blueberries
1 tbsp fresh ginger, minced
2 tbsp apple cider vinegar
2 tbsp honey
1 tbsp butter

TOPPINGS

1 cup cream cheese

12 small brioche buns

PREPARATION

Combine lamb burger ingredients and form 12 small patties. Refrigerate.

In a small pot, mix together chutney ingredients and reduce until thick.

Cook patties for 3 minutes on each side.

Toast brioche buns. Spread cream cheese on bun bottoms and top with patties and blueberry chutney. Serve.

 **DID YOU KNOW?**

Blueberries are rich in immunity-boosting anti-oxidants.

39

PORK SCHNITZEL BURGER

SERVES 4

TASTY TIP

Schnitzel and potato salad are a classic combination—why not try our decadent potato salad recipe in *The World's 60 Best Salads... Period*?

DID YOU KNOW?

Schnitzel is a traditional Austrian veal dish that can also be made with veal or chicken.

FOR PORK SCHNITZEL

4 pork cutlets (about 1/3 pound each)
1 tbsp fresh thyme, chopped
2 tbsp fresh parsley, chopped
1 clove garlic, minced
1 cup (250 ml) bread crumbs
Salt and freshly ground pepper
1 tbsp strong mustard (English or Dijon)
2 tbsp vegetable oil
Juice of 1/2 lemon

FOR HORSERADISH MAYONNAISE

3 tbsp mayonnaise
1 tbsp honey
1 tsp horseradish
4 drops Tabasco sauce

TOPPINGS

2 tomatoes, sliced
A few leaves iceberg lettuce

4 burger buns

PREPARATION

In a small bowl, combine mayonnaise, honey, horseradish, and Tabasco sauce.

In a bowl, mix together thyme, parsley, garlic, and bread crumbs. Season pork with salt and pepper, brush with mustard, and coat with bread crumb and herb mixture. Heat vegetable oil in a pan over medium heat and cook cutlets for 2 minutes on each side. Pour lemon juice over cooked schnitzel to finish.

Toast buns. Spread horseradish mayonnaise on bun bottoms and top with schnitzel, tomato slices, and iceberg lettuce. Serve.

40

GREEN & BLUE BURGER

SERVES 4

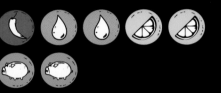

FOR BLUE CHEESE BURGERS

1 lb ground beef
1/4 cup (60 ml) blue cheese, crumbled
1 tbsp roasted garlic (see recipe on page 040)
1/2 onion, finely chopped
2 tbsp chives, chopped
Salt
1 tbsp freshly ground pepper

FOR APPLE ENDIVE SALAD

1 endive
1 green apple
1 tbsp olive oil
1 tsp sherry vinegar

FOR DIJONNAISE

2 tbsp mayonnaise
1 tsp Dijon mustard

TOPPINGS

4 small slices blue cheese

4 burger buns

PREPARATION

Combine blue cheese burger ingredients. Form 4 patties.

Cut endive in half lengthwise and discard the heart. Cut remaining leaves lengthwise into very thin strips. Julienne the apple and toss with endive, oil and vinegar.

Mix together mayonnaise and mustard.

Cook patties for 5 to 6 minutes on each side. Top with blue cheese 1 minute before removing from heat.

Toast buns. Spread Dijonnaise on bun bottoms. Top with patties and apple salad. Serve.

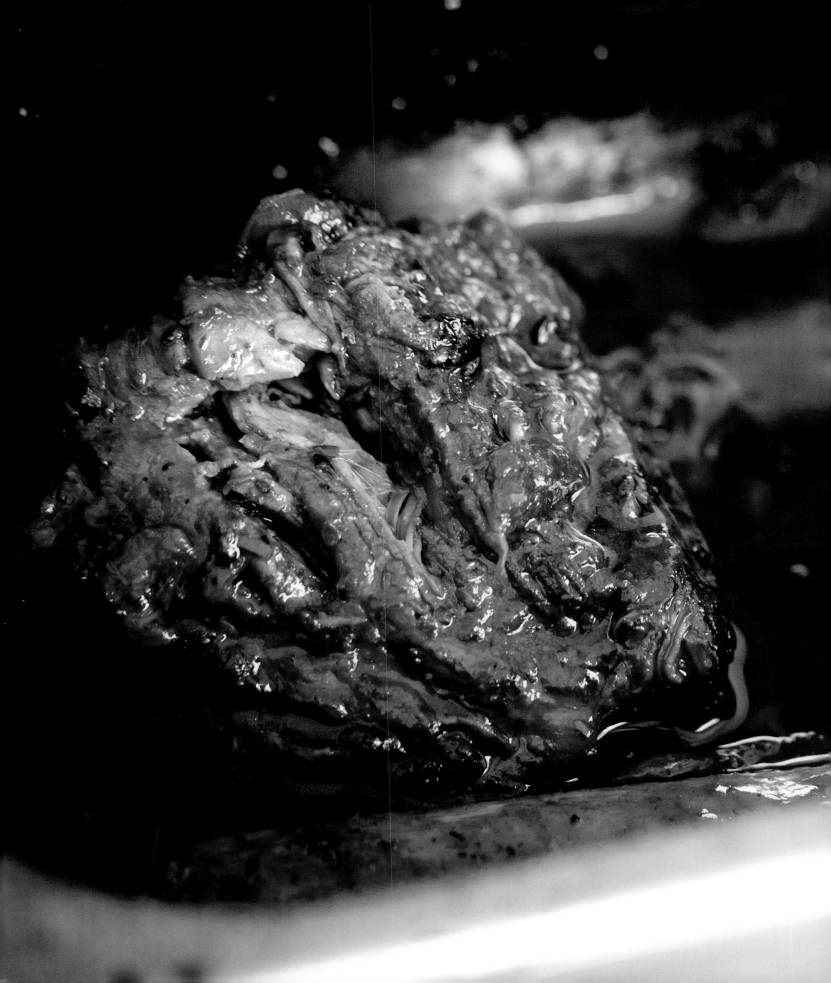

41

THE PORTUGUESE

ERVES 4

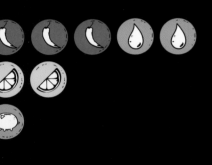

FOR BIFANA PORK

4 thin slices (about 1/4-inch) pork butt
2 tbsp Portuguese sweet red pepper paste (massa de pimentão)
4 cloves garlic, minced
3 bay leaves
1/4 cup (60 ml) white wine
1 tbsp lemon juice
Freshly ground pepper

FOR GARNISH

4 eggs
Salt and freshly ground pepper
2 tbsp vegetable oil
2 tbsp mayonnaise
4 slices tomato
1 small white onion, sliced into rounds
4 leaves lettuce
2 tbsp butter

4 Portuguese buns

PREPARATION

For marinade, combine red pepper paste, garlic, bay leaves, white wine, lemon juice, and pepper. Marinate pork for 24 hours.

In a bowl, beat eggs. Season with salt and pepper.

In a large non-stick pan, heat oil and pour in eggs. Cook until bottom begins to set. Flip, continue to cook, and then divide into 4 wedges. Keep warm.

Remove pork slices from marinade and cook for 2 to 3 minutes on each side.

Toast and butter both bun halves. Spread mayonnaise on bun bottoms. Top with pork, egg wedges, tomato slices, onion slices, and lettuce. Serve.

TASTY TIP

ayonnaise is easy to make at home!
ee recipe on page 032)

42

CHICKEN CURRY BURGER

SERVES 4

FOR CHICKEN BURGERS

1 lb ground chicken
1 tbsp olive oil
1 onion, finely chopped
2 tbsp 15% cream
1 tbsp chives, chopped
2 tbsp bread crumbs
1 tbsp lemongrass, chopped
Hot sauce, to taste
Salt and freshly ground pepper

FOR CURRY MAYONNAISE

1/4 cup (60 ml) mayonnaise
1 tbsp curry powder
1 tbsp lemon juice

GARNITURE

8 slices roasted red pepper (see recipe on page 034)
A few leaves iceberg lettuce

4 burger buns

PREPARATION

Cook onion in olive oil. Remove from heat and allow to cool slightly. Combine chicken burger ingredients. Form 4 patties and refrigerate.

In a bowl, mix together mayonnaise, curry, and lemon juice.

Cook patties for 7 to 8 minutes on each side.

Toast buns and top with patties, roasted red peppers, lettuce, and curry mayonnaise.

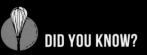

DID YOU KNOW?

Curry powder is a mixture of spices that usually includes coriander, cumin, turmeric, fenugreek, and red pepper. It is widely used in Indian, Pakistani, Bangladeshi, Sri Lankan, Thai, and other Southeast Asian cuisines.

43

BRAISED BEEF & RED WINE

SERVES 4

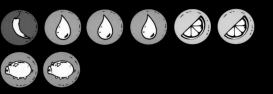

FOR SHORT RIBS

1 tbsp vegetable oil
2 beef short ribs, trimmed of fat
1 onion, finely chopped
2 cloves garlic, minced
1 tbsp tomato paste
1/2 cup (125 ml) red wine
2 sprigs fresh thyme
1 cup (250 ml) water
1 bay leaf
1 tbsp dried oregano

FOR BASIL ORANGE MAYONNAISE

4 tbsp (60 ml) mayonnaise
Zest of 1 orange and 1 tbsp juice
5 large fresh basil leaves, chopped

TOPPINGS

8 slices pickled beets

4 burger buns

PREPARATION

In a Dutch oven or heavy oven-safe cooking pot, heat oil over high heat and sear ribs on each side. Add onion, garlic, and tomato paste and cook until onions are golden brown. Deglaze with red wine.

Add remaining ingredients, cover, and cook in a 300°F (150°C) oven, about 3 hours or until the meat falls off the bone.

When the meat has finished cooking, remove bones and cut ribs in half. Reduce sauce until thick enough to thoroughly coat ribs.

In a bowl, combine mayonnaise ingredients.

Toast buns. Spread mayonnaise on bun bottoms and top with meat and sliced beets. Serve.

THE VIETNAMESE

SERVES 4

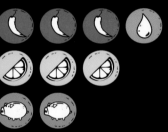

FOR BEEF BURGERS

1 lb ground beef
3 tbsp soy sauce
1 tbsp nuoc mam (Vietnamese fish sauce)
1 shallot, minced
1 clove garlic, minced
1 tbsp sambal oelek

FOR PICKLED CARROTS AND ONIONS

2 carrots, julienned
1 onion, thinly sliced
1/4 cup (60 ml) rice vinegar
1/4 cup (60 ml) water
2 tbsp sugar
Salt
1 tbsp nuoc mam

FOR SPICY GINGER MAYONNAISE

1/2 cup (125 ml) mayonnaise
1 tbsp fresh ginger, grated
2 tsp sambal oelek

TOPPINGS

A few leaves each of mint, cilantro, and Thai basil

4 burger buns

PREPARATION

In a small pot, heat rice vinegar, water, sugar, salt, and nuoc mam (fish sauce). Cook until sugar has dissolved, but do not bring to a boil. In a bowl, pour mixture over carrots and onions. Refrigerate for at least 2 hours.

Combine beef burger ingredients. Form 4 patties.

In another bowl, mix together mayonnaise, ginger, and sambal oelek.

Cook patties for 5 to 6 minutes on each side.

Toast buns. Drain liquid from pickled carrots and onions. Spread mayonnaise on bun bottoms and top with patties, pickled vegetables, and mint, cilantro, and Thai basil leaves. Serve.

TASTY TIP

Make your own traditional Vietnamese sandwiches (bánh mì) by serving these burgers on baguettes instead of buns!

VADA PAV BURGER

SERVES 4

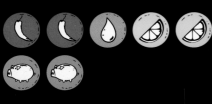

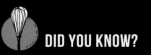 **DID YOU KNOW?**

Vada pav is a vegetarian fast food sandwich invented in the Indian state of Maharashtra.

FOR CILANTRO CHUTNEY

2 cups (500 ml) fresh cilantro, chopped
2 tbsp lemon juice
2 tbsp roasted peanuts
2 tbsp dried unsweetened coconut
1/2 jalapeño, seeded
Salt and freshly ground pepper

FOR TAMARIND CHUTNEY

1 cup (250 ml) tamarind paste
1 cup (250 ml) water
2 tsp fennel seeds
1 tsp crushed red pepper flakes
3/4 cup (180 ml) brown sugar
1/3 cup (80 ml) pitted dates

FOR VADA PAV

1 1/2 lbs russet potatoes (or any variety of starchy potato),
peeled, cooked and mashed
2 tsp wholegrain mustard
1/2-inch piece ginger, grated
2 cloves garlic, minced
1 tsp turmeric
1 small hot pepper, minced
1/4 cup (60 ml) fresh mint, chopped

FOR BATTER

1/2 cup (125 ml) plain yogurt
1 1/4 cup (310 ml) chickpea flour
1 tbsp ground coriander
1 tbsp ground cumin
1 tbsp baking powder
3/4 cup (180 ml) water
Vegetable oil for frying

PREPARATION

For cilantro chutney: In a food processor, combine cilantro chutney ingredients. Season and set aside.

For tamarind chutney: In a small pot, combine all tamarind chutney ingredients and simmer, uncovered, for 15 minutes. Blend in a food processor. Chutney should be thick but not completely smooth.

For vada pav: Combine vada pav patty ingredients. Form 4 patties. Refrigerate. In a bowl, whisk together batter ingredients. To cook, dip patties in batter and fry in oil until golden brown. To serve, spread tamarind chutney on bun bottoms. Top with vada pav patties and cilantro chutney.

VOLCANO BURGER

SERVES 4

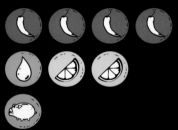

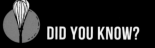

DID YOU KNOW?

Instead of reaching for a glass of water to cool your tongue after eating spicy food, nibble on a bit of oil-soaked bread. The oil absorbs the spice, while water only spreads the heat.

FOR SPICY BEEF BURGERS

1 lb ground beef
2 cloves garlic, minced
1 jalapeño, seeded and minced
1 tbsp habañero hot sauce
1 tsp crushed red pepper flakes
2 tbsp cilantro, chopped
1 tsp ground cumin

FOR PICKLED JALAPEÑOS

8 jalapeño peppers
2 cups white wine vinegar
1 tbsp salt
3 tbsp sugar
1 tsp coriander seeds
1 tbsp peppercorns
1 tsp fennel seeds
1 tsp mustard seeds

TOPPINGS

4 slices pepper jack cheese
Choice of condiments

4 hamburger buns

PREPARATION

For pickled jalapeños: With a small knife, make a cut down the center of each jalapeño pepper. In a pot, combine remaining ingredients, bring to a boil, and continue boiling for 2 minutes. Pour mixture over jalapeños and cover. Refrigerate for 48 hours. Drain and thinly slice before serving.

Combine spicy burger ingredients. Form 4 patties.

Cook patties for 5 to 6 minutes on each side. Top with cheese and allow cheese to melt.

Toast buns and top with patties, pickled jalapeños, and your favorite condiments.

47

MINI TURKEY BURGERS WITH GUACAMOLE

MAKES 12 MINI BURGERS

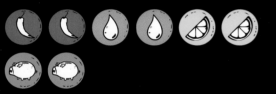

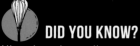

FOR TURKEY BURGERS

1 lb ground turkey
Salt and freshly ground pepper

FOR GUACAMOLE

2 ripe avocados
Juice of 1 lime
1/4 cup (60 ml) fresh cilantro, chopped
2 tbsp olive oil
1 jalapeño, seeded and minced
2 tomatoes, seeded and diced

TOPPINGS

3 slices cheddar cheese, cut into 4 to make 12 squares
6 slices bacon, cooked and cut into 4 pieces each

24 mini pitas

PREPARATION

In a bowl, mash avocado with a fork. Combine with remaining guacamole ingredients, adding tomatoes last.

Combine burger ingredients and form 12 small patties.

Cook patties for 3 minutes on one side. Flip patties, add cheese, and cook for another 3 minutes. Top with bacon.

Toast pitas and top with patties. Spoon 1 tbsp guacamole onto each burger and serve.

DID YOU KNOW?
Historians have discovered that the Aztecs were making guacamole as early as the 16th century!

48

DUCK & FOIE GRAS

SERVES 4

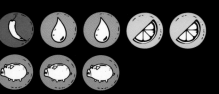

FOR DUCK BURGERS

1 lb duck, ground or chopped by hand
5 prunes, pitted and chopped
1 tsp ground Espelette pepper
2 tbsp bread crumbs
Salt and freshly ground pepper

FOR CARAMELIZED ONIONS WITH ANISE

2 onions, thinly sliced
1 tbsp butter
2 tbsp raspberry vinegar
1 star anise
1/2 cup (125 ml) water
Salt and freshly ground pepper

FOR GARNISH

4 slices foie gras *au torchon*
1 handful arugula

4 brioche buns

PREPARATION

Mix together duck burger ingredients. Form 4 patties.

In a small pot, brown onions in butter and then deglaze with raspberry vinegar. Add star anise and water; cover and cook for 5 minutes. Uncover, season with salt and pepper, and reduce until liquid has completely evaporated. Discard star anise.

Cook duck patties for 4 to 5 minutes on each side.

Toast buns and top with patties, foie gras, caramelized onions, and arugula.

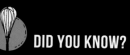

DID YOU KNOW?

spelette peppers were originally used medici-
ally, but became popular for conserving meat
d preparing condiments. It is now a staple of
asque cuisine!

TURKEY & SWEET POTATO

SERVES 4

 **DID YOU KNOW?**

Brie has been produced in France since the 8th century, while Camembert only appeared in the 19th century.

FOR TURKEY BURGERS

2 sweet potatoes, peeled, boiled and cubed
1 lb ground turkey
1/2 red onion, finely chopped
Salt and freshly ground pepper
1 tsp ground cumin
1 tsp ground cardamom
1 tsp vegetable oil
1 jalapeño, seeded and minced
1/4 cup (60 ml) bread crumbs

FOR MAYONNAISE

1/4 cup (60 ml) mayonnaise
1/4 cup (60 ml) ketchup
Zest and juice of 1 lime

TOPPINGS

8 slices brie or camembert cheese
1 handful baby spinach

4 burger buns

PREPARATION

Combine turkey burger ingredients. Form 4 patties.

Cook patties in a 400°F (200°C) oven for 20 minutes. Top with cheese 1 minute before removing from oven.

Combine mayonnaise ingredients.

Toast buns. Spread mayonnaise on bun bottoms and top with patties and baby spinach. Serve.

BURGER WITH CREAMY ARTICHOKE SPREAD

SERVES 4

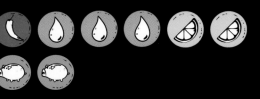

FOR BEEF AND PORK BURGERS

1/2 lb ground beef
1/2 lb ground pork
2 tbsp steak spice
1 onion, finely chopped
2 tbsp bread crumbs
1 egg
2 tbsp ketchup

FOR ARTICHOKE SPREAD

1/4 cup (60 ml) cream cheese
2 tbsp mayonnaise
2 tbsp fresh Parmesan cheese, grated
2 tbsp fresh Monterey jack cheese, grated
1 tbsp hot sauce
1 tsp Worcestershire sauce
Salt and freshly ground pepper
4 canned or jarred artichoke hearts in water,
drained and roughly chopped
1 green onion, thinly sliced

4 burger buns

PREPARATION

Combine beef and pork burger ingredients. Form 4 patties.

In a food processor, mix together cream cheese, mayonnaise, Parmesan, Monterey jack, hot sauce, and Worcestershire sauce. Season with salt and pepper.

Transfer cheese and mayonnaise mixture to a bowl and stir in artichokes and green onion. Microwave for 30 seconds before assembling burgers.

Cook patties for 5 to 6 minutes on each side.

Toast buns and top with patties and artichoke spread.

RINGSIDE BURGER WITH PORT SAUCE

SERVES 4

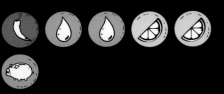

FOR BEEF BURGERS

1 lb ground beef
2 tbsp steak spice
2 tbsp ketchup
2 tbsp bread crumbs
1 egg
2 tbsp shallots or chives, minced

FOR PORT SAUCE

1 tbsp butter
2 medium shallots, sliced
2 cloves garlic, sliced
2 sprigs fresh thyme
1 bay leaf
1 cup (250 ml) port
1 cup (250 ml) store-bought veal or beef demi-glace
1 tbsp butter

TOPPINGS

20 store-bought onion rings
1/2 cup goat cheese

4 onion buns

PREPARATION

For port sauce : In a small pot, sauté shallots, garlic, thyme, and bay leaf in 1 tbsp butter. Add port and reduce by half. Remove from heat and strain with a mesh strainer into a larger pot. Add demi-glace and reduce until sauce is thick. Remove from heat and add remaining 1 tbsp butter, whisking constantly until fully incorporated. Keep warm.

Combine beef burger ingredients and form 4 patties.

Cook patties for 5 to 6 minutes on each side. Brush with port sauce halfway through cooking.

Cook onion rings according to package directions.

Toast buns. Top with patties, crumbled goat cheese, fried onion rings, and port sauce. Serve.

 **TASTY TIP**

If you're looking for something a little different, spread a bit of pepper or cranberry goat cheese on your burger!

THE MEXICAN

SERVES 4

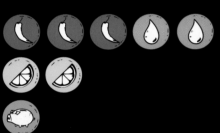

DID YOU KNOW?

In Mexico, over 40 different varieties of chili peppers are used in everyday cooking!

FOR BEEF BURGERS

1 tbsp vegetable oil
1 small onion, finely chopped
1/2 cup (125 ml) red kidney beans
1/2 cup (125 ml) corn
1 tbsp cumin
3/4 lb ground beef
2 tbsp fresh cilantro, chopped
1 egg
2 tbsp bread crumbs
1/4 chipotle pepper in adobo sauce, chopped
Salt and freshly ground pepper

TOPPINGS

4 slices Monterey jack cheese
4 slices tomato
1 avocado, diced
A few banana pepper rings
2 tbsp sour cream

4 burger buns

PREPARATION

In a pan, heat vegetable oil and cook onion, beans and corn. Add cumin 30 seconds before removing from heat. Transfer to a bowl and combine with remaining burger ingredients. Form 4 patties.

Cook patties for 5 to 6 minutes on each side and top with Monterey Jack cheese. Allow cheese to melt.

Toast buns. Top with patties, tomato slices, avocado, banana peppers, and sour cream. Serve.

RACLETTE BURGER

SERVES 4

FOR BEEF BURGERS

1 lb ground beef
1 egg
2 tbsp steak spice
2 tbsp bread crumbs
2 tbsp ketchup
2 tbsp shallots or chives, minced
1 tbsp fresh thyme, chopped
Salt and freshly ground pepper

FOR MUSHROOMS WITH RED WINE

1 tbsp butter
16 button mushrooms, sliced
Salt and freshly ground pepper
3/4 cup (180 ml) red wine
6 sage leaves, chopped
2 tbsp butter

TOPPINGS

4 slices raclette cheese

4 hamburger buns

PREPARATION

Combine all beef burger ingredients and form 4 patties. Refrigerate.

In a pan, sauté mushrooms in 1 tbsp butter until lightly browned. Season with salt and pepper. Deglaze with red wine, add sage, and reduce until liquid has evaporated.

Remove from heat and add remaining 2 tbsp butter, stirring until mushrooms are coated in a velvety sauce. Keep warm.

Cook patties for 5 to 6 minutes on each side. Top patties with raclette 1 minute before removing from heat.

Toast buns and top with patties and mushrooms. Serve.

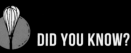 **DID YOU KNOW?**

Raclette is actually a traditional Swiss dish. Raclette cheese is heated, scraped onto plates, and served with small potatoes, dried meat, gherkins, and pickled onions.

THE ITALIAN

SERVES 4

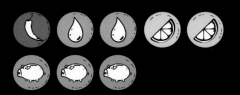

DID YOU KNOW?

Italians consume 160 million kilos of mozzarella every month!

FOR VEAL BURGERS

1 lb ground veal
1 egg
2 tbsp bread crumbs
2 tbsp steak spice
Salt and freshly ground pepper
2 tbsp grated Parmesan cheese
2 tbsp shallots or chives, minced

FOR BASIL MAYONNAISE

6 basil leaves
1 tbsp olive oil
2 tbsp mayonnaise
1 tsp lemon juice

TOPPINGS

4 slices eggplant
8 slices pancetta
1 ball fresh mozzarella, sliced into rounds
4 slices tomato

4 burger buns

PREPARATION

Combine veal burger ingredients. Form 4 patties.

In a small food processor, purée basil and olive oil. Add mayonnaise and lemon juice.

Cook patties for 5 to 6 minutes on each side.

Brush eggplant slices with oil and cook for 30 seconds on each side. Quickly fry pancetta, about 30 seconds.

Toast buns. Spread a bit of mayonnaise on bun bottoms and top with patties, pancetta, mozzarella, eggplant, tomato, and more mayonnaise.

FALAFEL BURGER

SERVES 4

FOR FALAFELS

1 can chickpeas, drained and rinsed
1 onion, chopped
2 cloves garlic
1/2 cup (125 ml) fresh parsley
1/2 cup (125 ml) fresh cilantro
2 tbsp ground cumin
2 tbsp ground coriander
Salt and freshly ground pepper
1 tbsp crushed red pepper flakes
1 tbsp baking powder
6 tbsp flour
1/2 cup (125 ml) water
Vegetable oil for frying

FOR TAHINI SAUCE

1/4 cup (60 ml) tahini
1/4 cup (60 ml) water
Juice of 1 lemon
Salt and freshly ground pepper

TOPPINGS

1 tomato, cut into small dice
1/4 cup (60 ml) fresh parsley, chopped
2 tbsp olive oil
1 tbsp lemon juice
Salt and freshly ground pepper

4 burger buns

PREPARATION

In a food processor, purée chickpeas, onion, garlic, parsley and cilantro. Add water as needed.

In a large bowl, combine all falafel ingredients except oil and mix well.

Heat oil in a pan. Form 6 balls (about 2 tbsp each) and fry until golden brown, about 4 minutes. Repeat with remaining mixture.

In a bowl, mix together tomatoes, parsley, olive oil, and lemon juice. Season with salt and pepper.

Combine tahini sauce ingredients.

Toast buns and top with falafels, tahini sauce, and tomato and parsley mixture.

THE STEAMROLLER

SERVES 4

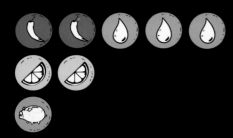

FOR BEEF BURGERS

1 lb ground beef
2 tsp steak spice
1 tbsp ketchup

FOR PICKLED ONIONS

1/4 cup (60 ml) water
1/4 cup (60 ml) lime juice
1/2 cup (125 ml) white vinegar
2 tbsp sugar
2 tbsp salt
2 red onions, thinly sliced
1 tbsp dried oregano
1 jalapeño, seeded and minced

FOR BROWN SAUCE

1 cup store-bought gravy
1 tbsp paprika
1 tbsp Dijon mustard
1 tsp hot sauce
Freshly ground pepper

TOPPING

8 slices Swiss cheese

8 burger buns

PREPARATION

For pickled onions : In a pot, bring water, lime juice, vinegar, sugar and salt to a boil. Add onions, oregano and jalapeño. Cover and refrigerate for 24 hours.

In a pot, whisk together sauce ingredients and boil for 5 minutes.

Combine burger ingredients and form 4 patties. Cook for 5 to 6 minutes on each side.

Drain onions. Top buns with cheese slices, patties, pickled onions, and a bit of sauce. Reserve remaining sauce.

In a pan, flatten burgers using a large spatula. Cook until buns are golden brown and crispy. Serve reserved sauce on the side for dipping.

MUSHROOM BARBECUE BURGER

SERVES 4

FOR BEEF BURGERS

1 lb ground beef
2 tbsp shallots, minced
1 tsp Worcestershire sauce
2 tbsp barbecue sauce (see recipe on page 036)
2 tbsp bread crumbs
1 egg

TOPPINGS

2 portobello mushrooms, thickly sliced
2 white onions, sliced
2 tbsp butter
1/4 cup (60 ml) barbecue sauce (see recipe on page 036)
Salt and freshly ground pepper
4 slices yellow or orange cheddar

4 burger buns

PREPARATION

Combine all beef burger ingredients. Form 4 patties.

In a pan, sauté mushrooms and onions in butter over high heat. Add barbecue sauce and season with salt and pepper.

Cook patties for 5 to 6 minutes on each side. Top with cheddar cheese and allow cheese to melt.

Toast buns. Top with patties and sautéed mushrooms and onions.

TWO-IN-ONE BURGER

SERVES 4

FOR BURGERS

1 recipe for Classic Burgers (see recipe on page 032)

FOR THE ULTIMATE FRENCH FRIES

4 large russet potatoes, peeled
Vegetable oil for frying
Salt

TOPPINGS

Ketchup
Choice of condiments

4 burger buns

PREPARATION

Cut potatoes into 1/2-inch thick sticks. Soak in cold water for at least 1 hour.

In a deep pot with a heavy base or in a deep fryer, heat oil to 325°F (160°C).

Drain potatoes and dry well. Deep-fry in small batches, about 4 minutes per batch. Drain on paper towels.

Increase the heat of the oil to 375°F (190°C) and refry potatoes in small batches until golden brown, about 3 or 4 minutes per batch. Drain on paper towels and season immediately.

Cook patties. Toast buns and top with patties, ketchup, French fries, and your favorite condiments.

TASTY TIP

Serve up some Belgian *mitraillettes*! Just top demi-baguettes with patties, fries, and your choice of condiments.

THE MOROCCAN

SERVES 4

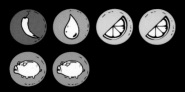

FOR BEEF MERGUEZ BURGERS

1/2 lb ground beef
1/2 lb merguez sausage meat
Zest of 1 lemon
2 tbsp shallots, finely chopped
Salt and freshly ground pepper

FOR FETA SPREAD

1/2 cup (125 ml) feta cheese
1 tbsp plain Greek yogurt
2 tbsp fresh mint, chopped
2 tbsp fresh cilantro, chopped
2 tbsp olive oil
Juice of 1 lemon
1 clove garlic, finely chopped

FOR TOMATO OLIVE GARNISH

2 tomatoes, seeded and cut into small dice
12 pitted black olives, chopped
1 tbsp olive oil
Salt and freshly ground pepper

4 burger buns

PREPARATION

Combine burger ingredients. Form 4 patties and refrigerate.

In a food processor, combine all feta spread ingredients except garlic. Stir chopped garlic into feta mixture at the very end.

In a food processor, pulse tomatoes and olives together for a few seconds. Add oil and season with salt and pepper.

Cook patties for 5 to 6 minutes on each side.

Toast buns and top with patties, feta spread, and tomato and olive mixture. Serve.

THE EMPIRE BURGER

SERVES 4

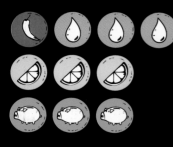

🍴 TASTY TIP

Here's how *we* suggest you assemble your burger to avoid getting messy. Get creative and try out your own combinations! Good luck!

01. BUN
02. KETCHUP
03. CARAMELIZED ONIONS
04. PATTY
05. CHEDDAR CHEESE
06. PICKLES
07. MAYONNAISE
08. BUN
09. MUSTARD
10. TOMATO
11. PATTY
12. SWISS CHEESE
13. BACON
14. LETTUCE
15. BANANA PEPPERS
16. BUTTER
17. BUN

FOR BURGERS

1 double recipe for classic burgers (see recipe on page 032)

TOPPINGS

4 slices cheddar cheese
4 slices Swiss cheese
4 slices bacon, cooked
4 slices tomato
1/2 cup (125 ml) caramelized onions (see recipe on page 044)
4 tbsp mayonnaise
4 dill pickles, sliced
4 tbsp mustard
4 tbsp ketchup
8 banana pepper rings
4 leaves lettuce

6 burger buns
4 tbsp butter

PREPARATION

Make 8 beef patties (following the Classic Burger recipe).

Cook patties for 5 to 6 minutes on each side and top 4 with cheddar and 4 with Swiss cheese 1 minute before removing from heat.

Now it's time to stack the burgers. Always remember that the key to successful stacked burgers is proper assembly!

Make sure to layer all ingredients that might slide off the burgers (pickles, tomatoes and condiments) between ingredients that will help keep them in place.

INGREDIENTS INDEX

A

ALLSPICE...068, 120
ALMONDS...118
APPLE, GREEN...044, 108, 124
ARTICHOKES...148
ARUGULA............................070, 098, 108, 110, 144
AVOCADO...142, 154

B

BABA GHANOUSH..118
BACON..............032, 048, 052, 074, 080, 100, 112, 142, 172
BAKING POWDER..136, 160
BARBECUE SAUCE....................036, 038, 076, 084, 166
BASIL...132, 156
BASIL PESTO..070
BASIL, THAI..134
BAY LEAVES.......................................128, 132, 152
BEANS, BLACK...082
BEANS, RED KIDNEY...154
BEEF......032, 036, 046, 052, 072, 076, 080, 084, 110, 116, 124,
.......132, 134, 140, 148, 152, 154, 156, 164, 166, 168, 170, 172
BEER...088, 096
BEETS, PICKLED...080, 132
BLUEBERRIES..120

C

CAPERS...050
CARDAMOM..146
CARROTS...038, 118, 134
CAYENNE PEPPER...112
CHEESE, BLUE...112, 124
CHEESE, BRIE...146
CHEESE, CAMEMBERT...146
CHEESE, CHEDDAR.........032, 044, 074, 080, 110, 142, 166, 172
CHEESE, EMMENTAL..096

CHEESE, FETA 106, 170
CHEESE, GOAT 034, 040, 070, 110, 152
CHEESE, MONTEREY JACK 094, 148, 154
CHEESE, MOZZARELLA 104, 158
CHEESE, OLD CHEDDAR 052, 088
CHEESE, PARMESAN 060, 082, 104, 110, 148, 158
CHEESE, PEPPER JACK 140
CHEESE, RACLETTE 156
CHEESE, REBLOCHON 048
CHEESE, SHEEP'S MILK 118
CHEESE, SMOKED (GOUDA) 076
CHEESE, SWISS 110, 164, 172
CHICKEN 060, 068, 086, 104, 130
CHICKEN BOUILLON CUBE 060
CHICKPEA FLOUR 136
CHICKPEAS 160
CHILI POWDER 036
CHILI SAUCE 064
CHIVES .. 032, 034, 040, 048, 050, 052, 080, 110, 112, 130, 152,
.... 156, 158, 168, 172
CHUTNEY (STORE-BOUGHT) 108
CELERY 098, 108
CILANTRO 058, 064, 076, 100, 106, 134, 136, 140, 142, 154,
.... 160, 170
COCONUT 136
COD 098
COFFEE 076
CORIANDER SEEDS 140
CORN 092, 154
CRAB 092
CREAM, 15 % 130
CREAM, 35 % 118
CREAM CHEESE 040, 064, 120, 148
CRUSHED RED PEPPER FLAKES 056, 062, 136, 140, 160
CUCUMBER 086

CUMIN 058, 062, 082, 092, 136, 140, 146, 154
CURRY 130

D

DATES 136
DEMI-GLACE 116, 152, 164
DUCK 108, 144

E

EGGPLANT 070, 158
EGGS 074, 080
ENDIVE 024
ESPELETTE PEPPER 144

F

FENNEL SEEDS 136, 140
FOIE GRAS 116, 144

G

GARAM MASALA 118
GARLIC .. 036, 040, 048, 056, 058, 060, 062, 064, 068, 070, 072,
...... 076, 082, 084, 100, 104, 108, 110, 122, 124, 128, 132, 134,
.... 136, 140, 152, 160, 170
GARLIC POWDER 038
GINGER 100, 120, 134, 136
GREEN CABBAGE 038, 068

H

HABANERO SAUCE 140
HAM 088
HARISSA SAUCE 060, 098
HAZELNUTS 108
HONEY 108, 120, 122
HORSERADISH 122
HOT SAUCE 130, 148, 164

K

KETCHUP 032, 036, 046, 072, 080, 110, 112, 146, 148, 152, 156, 160, 168, 172

L

LAMB 034, 040, 112, 118, 120
LEMON ...032, 046, 050, 060, 072, 082, 086, 092, 100, 104, 122, 128, 130, 136, 158, 160, 170
LEMONGRASS 130
LETTUCE 046, 060, 128, 172
LETTUCE, FRISÉE 048
LETTUCE, ICEBERG 062, 080, 122, 130
LIME 058, 062, 094, 098, 106, 142, 146, 164
LIQUID SMOKE 036, 038

M

MACE 068
MESCLUN 108
MILK 112
MINT 050, 086, 136, 170
MOLASSES 036
MUSHROOMS, BUTTON 040, 064, 156
MUSHROOMS, PORTOBELLO 070, 166
MUSHROOMS, SHIITAKE 082
MUSTARD, DIJON 032, 038, 040, 044, 046, 070, 088, 096, 122, 124, 164
MUSTARD, DRIED 038, 062
MUSTARD SEEDS 140
MUSTARD, WHOLEGRAIN 092, 096, 136

N

NUOC MAM (VIETNAMESE FISH SAUCE) 134
NUTMEG 068

O

OLIVES, BLACK 170

ONION, GREEN 068, 092, 100, 148
ONION, RED 064, 068, 070, 108, 146, 164
ONION RINGS (STORE-BOUGHT) 152
ORANGE 058, 068, 132
OREGANO 048, 076, 104, 132, 164

P

PANCETTA 040, 158
PAPRIKA 038, 056, 060, 062, 082, 084, 092, 164
PARSLEY 044, 046, 056, 072, 094, 122, 160
PEANUTS 136
PEAS, GREEN 050
PEPPERS, BANANA 154, 172
PEPPERS, CHIPOTLE 154
PEPPERS, GREEN 084
PEPPERS, GUAJILLO 058
PEPPERS, HABANERO 068
PEPPERS, HOT 136
PEPPERS, JALAPEÑO 094, 106, 136, 140, 142, 146, 164
PEPPERS, RED 034, 070, 092, 100, 130
PEPPERS, YELLOW 062
PICKLES 032, 038, 046, 050, 172
PINEAPPLE 058, 100
PIRI-PIRI SAUCE 034
PORK 038, 044, 058, 088, 094, 100, 122, 128, 148
PORT 152
PORT, WHITE 116
PORTUGUESE SWEET RED PEPPER PASTE 128
POTATO CHIPS 112
POTATOES 082, 098
POTATOES, RUSSET 136, 168
POTATOES, SWEET 146
PROSCUITTO 056
PRUNES 144

R

RAS EL HANOUT 086
ROSEMARY 040, 070

S

SAFFRON 062
SAGE 156
SALMON 106
SAMBAL OELEK 134
SAUERKRAUT 096
SAUSAGE, MILD 074, 096
SAUSAGE, MERGUEZ 170
SHALLOT 032, 036, 050, 052, 062, 072, 080, 098, 100, 106,
.................................110, 112, 134, 152, 156, 158, 166, 168, 170, 172
SHRIMP 062, 100
SOUR CREAM 094, 154
SOY SAUCE 100, 134
SPINACH 064, 106, 146
STAR ANISE 144
SUGAR, BROWN 036, 062, 068, 076, 136, 172
SUGAR, WHITE 038, 048, 134, 140, 160

T

TABASCO SAUCE 036, 046, 084, 092, 098, 100, 122
TAHINI 160
TAMARIND PASTE 136
TARRAGON 098
THYME 038, 060, 062, 068, 076, 122, 132, 152, 156
TILAPIA 056
TOFU 064
TOMATO 032, 040, 046, 048, 060, 074, 080, 086, 110, 118,
.................................122, 128, 142, 154, 158, 160, 170, 172
TOMATO, CHERRY 056, 092
TOMATO PASTE 036, 064, 084, 132
TOMATO SAUCE 084, 104

TOMATO, SUNDRIED 064
TRUFFLE 116
TRUFFLE PASTE 116
TURBOT 050
TURKEY 142, 146
TURMERIC 136
TZATZIKI 086

V

VEAL 048, 158
VINEGAR, APPLE CIDER 038, 120
VINEGAR, BALSAMIC 064, 070
VINEGAR, RASPBERRY 144
VINEGAR, RED WINE 036, 056, 156
VINEGAR, RICE 134
VINEGAR, SHERRY 044, 086, 108, 116, 124, 172
VINEGAR, WHITE WINE 044, 058, 140, 164

W

WHISKEY 036
WINE, MADEIRA 116
WINE, RED 108, 132
WINE, WHITE 128

Y

YOGURT 136
YOGURT, GREEK 170

Z

ZUCCHINI 070, 094

SAUCES, SPREADS, GARNISHES & SIDES

CARAMELIZED ONIONS..044

CARAMELIZED ONIONS WITH ANISE.................................144

CHIMICHURRI...056

CHUTNEY, BLUEBERRY..120

CHUTNEY, CILANTRO...136

CHUTNEY, TAMARIND...136

COLESLAW..068

COLESLAW, CREAMY..038

FRENCH FRIES..168

FRIED SHALLOTS..032

GARLIC BUTTER..072, 104

GREEN APPLE SLAW..044

GUACAMOLE...142

JALAPEÑO SOUR CREAM...094

MAYONNAISE, BASIL...158

MAYONNAISE, BASIL ORANGE......................................132

MAYONNAISE, CUMIN...092

MAYONNAISE, CURRY...130

MAYONNAISE, DIJON (DIJONNAISE)...........................044, 124

MAYONNAISE, HARISSA...098

MAYONNAISE, HOMEMADE..032

MAYONNAISE, HORSERADISH.......................................122

MAYONNAISE, LIME..106

MAYONNAISE, SAFFRON...062

MAYONNAISE, SPICY GINGER......................................134

MUSHROOMS WITH RED WINE.......................................156

PICKLED CARROTS AND ONIONS 134

PICKLED JALAPEÑOS 140

PICKLED ONIONS 164

PINEAPPLE SALSA 100

ROASTED ONIONS WITH THYME AND GARLIC 076

SALAD, APPLE ENDIVE 124

SALAD, CUCUMBER 086

SAUCE, BLUE CHEESE 112

SAUCE, MADEIRA DEMI-GLACE 116

SAUCE, PORT 152

SAUCE, WELSH RAREBIT 088

SAUCE, WHISKEY BARBECUE 036

SPREAD, FETA CHEESE 170

SPREAD, ROASTED GARLIC CHEESE 040

SPREAD, ARTICHOKE 148

TAHINI SAUCE 160

TARTAR SAUCE 050

TOMATO COMPOTE 048

TOMATO OLIVE GARNISH 170

TOMATO PARSLEY GARNISH 160

CONVERSION CHART

1 dl .... 10 cl .... 100 ml
1 tablespoon .... 15 ml
1 teaspoon .... 5 ml
1 oz .... 30 ml
1 cup .... 250 ml
4 cups .... 1 l
1/2 cup .... 125 ml
1/4 cup .... 60 ml
1/3 cup .... 80 ml
1 lb .... 450 g
2 lbs .... 900 g
2,2 lbs .... 1 kg
400°F .... 200°C T/7
350°F .... 175°C T/6
300°F .... 150°C T/5

Volume Conversion
* Approximate values

---

1 cup (250 ml) crumbled cheese .... 150 g
1 cup (250 ml) all-purpose flour .... 115 g
1 cup (250 ml) white sugar .... 200 g
1 cup (250 ml) brown sugar .... 220 g
1 cup (250 ml) butter .... 230 g
1 cup (250 ml) oil .... 215 g
1 cup (250 ml) canned tomatoes .... 250 g

NOTES

IN THE SAME COLLECTION

THE WORLD'S **60** BEST
SALADS
PERIOD.

THE WORLD'S **60** BEST
PASTA SAUCES
PERIOD.